New Longman Shakespeare

Macbeth

William Shakespeare

edited by John O'Connor

 LONGMAN

Pearson Education Limited
Edinburgh Gate
Harlow
Essex
CM20 2JE
England and Associated Companies throughout the World

ISBN 0582 36580 5

First published 1999
Printed in Singapore

The Publisher's policy is to use paper manufactured from
sustainable forests.

Acknowledgements

We are grateful to the following for permission to reproduce
photographs:

Front cover: Columbia Pictures/The Ronald Grant Archive
Mary Evans Picture Library/Utrecht University Library
(page 196); Paul Mulcahy (page 180); Shakespeare Centre
Library, Stratford-upon-Avon (pages 98, 148); Shakespeare
Centre Library/Joe Cocks Studio Collection (pages 12, 42, 78,
107); Shakespeare Centre Library/Malcolm Davies (pages 52,
122, 126); Shakespeare Centre Library/Mark Douet (pages 118,
170) Ian Tilton (pages 46, 108, 176); John Tramper (page 197).

Contents

Introduction

To the student

Shakespeare wrote *Macbeth* so that it could be performed by actors and enjoyed by audiences. To help you get the most out of the play, this edition includes:
- a complete **script**;
- **notes** printed next to the script which explain difficulties and point out important features;
- **activities** on the same page which will help you to focus on the scene you are reading;
- page-by-page **summaries** of the plot;
- **exam questions** after each Act, which will give you practice at the right level;
- **background information** about *Macbeth*, Shakespeare's theatre and the verse he uses; and
- **advice** on how to set out titles and quotations in your essays.

To the teacher

New Longman Shakespeare has been designed to meet the varied and complex needs of students working throughout the 11–16 age-range.

The textual notes

These have been newly written to provide understandable explanations which are easily located on the page:
- notes are placed next to the text with clear line references
- explanations of more complex words are given in context and help is provided with key imagery and historical references.

The activities

1 **Activities accompanying the text**

There are based on the premise that the text is best enjoyed and understood as a script for performance:

- In addition to a wide variety of reading, writing, listening and speaking activities, students are encouraged to: improvise, learn the script for performance, freeze-frame, rehearse, hot-seat, devise graphs and charts and create various forms of artwork, including storyboards, collages and cartoons.
- To provide a clear structure, activities are placed opposite the section of text to which they refer and come under five headings:
  - **i Character reviews** help students to think about the many different aspects of a given character which are presented in the course of the play. There might be as many as twenty of these activities on a single major character.
  - **ii Actors' interpretations** draw upon actual performances and ask students to consider comments from actors and directors in film and stage productions.
  - **iii Shakespeare's language** activities, focusing on everything from imagery to word-play, enable students to understand how the dramatist's language works to convey the central ideas of the play.
  - **iv Plot reviews** help students to keep in mind the essential details of what is happening in the story as well as asking them to consider how the plot is structured.
  - **v Themes** are explored according to their predominance in each play.
- 'Serial activities' (Macbeth 1, ... 2, ... 3, for example) enable students to focus in detail on a single key feature.

In addition, students who find extended tasks on Shakespeare a daunting prospect can combine several of these more focused activities – each in itself free-standing – to form the basis of a fuller piece of work.

2 Exam-style activities

At the end of each Act – and also at the end of the book – there are activities which require SATs and GCSE style responses and offer opportunities for assessment.

3 Summative activities

Thinking about the play as a whole ... is a section which offers a wide range of summative activities suitable for all levels.

Differentiation
Many students using this edition will be approaching Shakespeare for the first time; some might be studying the play for their Key Stage 3 SATs exam; others will be working towards GCSE.

Introduction

To answer their very different needs and interests, many of the activities have been differentiated to match the National Curriculum Level Descriptions and GCSE criteria. Activities of this kind are presented in three levels:

A Foundation level activities, which support an initial reading of the play and help students to build a solid basic knowledge and understanding.
B Activities geared towards the needs of Year 9 Key Stage 3 students preparing for SATs.
C More advanced activities in line with GCSE requirements.

Plot summaries

As students work through the play, their understanding of the play's plot is supported by:
• a brief headline summary at the top of each spread
• regular Plot Review activities
• a final detailed summary, scene by scene.

Background

Details are provided on:
• Shakespeare's England
• Plays and playhouses
• The Globe theatre
• The social and historical background (to each particular play)
• Shakespeare's life and his times

Studying and writing about the play

To help students who are studying the play for examinations, there are sections on:
• Shakespeare's verse (with examples from the particular play)
• Study skills: titles and quotations

Characters in the play

In Scotland

DUNCAN, King of Scotland
MALCOLM, his elder son
DONALBAIN, his younger son
a wounded CAPTAIN in Duncan's army

MACBETH, a general in the King's army, Thane of Glamis
LADY MACBETH, his wife
SEYTON, Macbeth's armourer
a DOCTOR in Macbeth's castle
Lady Macbeth's GENTLEWOMAN
a PORTER
three MURDERERS
an ATTENDANT
a SERVANT
a MESSENGER

BANQUO, another general
FLEANCE, his son

MACDUFF, a Scottish nobleman, Thane of Fife
LADY MACDUFF, his wife
their SON
a MESSENGER
a MURDERER

LENOX
ROSSE   other
MENTETH   Scottish
ANGUS   noblemen
CATHNESS

three WITCHES
HECATE, the witch goddess
three APPARITIONS

an OLD MAN who talks with Rosse
a LORD who talks with Lenox

SIWARD, Earl of Northumberland

YOUNG SIWARD, his son

In England

a DOCTOR

and attendants, servants, messengers, lords, soldiers and
apparitions

*All the scenes are set in Scotland, apart from 4.3, which takes place in
the English court.*

1

1.1 A heath, somewhere in Scotland

A battle has taken place and three witches plan to meet Macbeth. In the Scottish camp, King Duncan asks for a report of the battle.

Activities

Actors' interpretations (1): the Witches

1. What do you know about witches and witchcraft? Brainstorm your knowledge and then read the section on page 200.
2. Act out scene 1 in groups of three (learn the lines first) and then discuss how you would present the Witches in a stage production. What should they look like and sound like? Are they old or young? How should they be dressed? How should they move and what actions should they perform?

Use your answers to these questions to rehearse and act out your own version of this first scene, bringing in whichever props and sound effects will make the scene come alive. Make sure you bring out these two important features of the scene:

- the fact that the Witches are planning to meet Macbeth
- that 'Fair is foul . . .' in their world and everything seems turned upside down.

3 **hurlyburly** confusion of the battle and the storm

5 **ere** before

8 **Graymalkin** 'grey little Mary': the Witches' cat

9 **Paddock** *a toad; Paddock and Graymalkin are the Witches' 'familiar spirits': demons in the form of animals*

Anon! At once! We're coming!

Exeunt *Latin for 'they leave'*

Alarm within *There is the sound of a battle-trumpet coming from 'inside' (in other words, just offstage).*

1–3 **He can report** . . . Judging by the bad condition he's in (**his plight**), he can report on the latest developments (**newest state**) of the rebellion (**revolt**).

4 **hardy** brave

5 **'Gainst my captivity** to save me from being captured

6 **knowledge of the broil** what you know about the conflict

7 **Doubtful** undecided

8 **spent** exhausted

Act 1

Scene 1

An open place.

Thunder and lightning. Enter THREE WITCHES.

1 WITCH	When shall we three meet again, In thunder, lightning or in rain?
2 WITCH	When the hurlyburly's done, When the battle's lost and won.
3 WITCH	That will be ere the set of sun.
1 WITCH	Where the place?
2 WITCH	Upon the heath.
3 WITCH	There to meet with Macbeth.
1 WITCH	I come, Graymalkin!
ALL	Paddock calls. – Anon! – Fair is foul, and foul is fair: Hover through the fog and filthy air.

5

10

Exeunt.

Scene 2

A camp near Forres.

Alarm within. Enter KING DUNCAN, MALCOLM, DONALBAIN,
LENOX, with attendants, meeting a bleeding CAPTAIN.

DUNCAN
(*To the lords*) What bloody man is that? He can report,
As seemeth by his plight, of the revolt
The newest state.

MALCOLM
This is the sergeant
Who, like a good and hardy soldier, fought
'Gainst my captivity. – (*To the soldier*) Hail, brave
   friend!   5
Say to the King the knowledge of the broil,
As thou didst leave it.

CAPTAIN
Doubtful it stood,
As two spent swimmers, that do cling together

3

1.2 A camp near Forres

A wounded soldier tells how Macbeth had killed the rebel Macdonwald and then, with Banquo, had fought off an attack from the Norwegians who were allied with the rebels.

Activities

Shakespeare's language: imagery (1)

To get across his ideas about the battle, the Captain uses a number of word pictures, or *images*.

A Find the images in lines 8–23 which help to convey the idea that:
- the battle was in the balance
- Macdonwald attracts bad qualities like flies
- luck is always changing sides
- Macbeth seemed like the pet or favourite of the god of courage.

B Pick one of the images in A and draw a cartoon or a picture (or find a photograph) which represents what you see in your mind's eye.

C Discuss what we learn about the nature of the battle that has just been fought. Then write notes on the ways in which the range of imagery in this first scene helps to make the account vivid. In addition to the images referred to in A, look at lines 22, 25–28 and 36–39.

9–13 **The merciless Macdonwald** – who makes a fitting rebel, because, to that end (**to that**), he has attracted all the natural evils (**multiplying villainies of nature**) – is being helped (**is supplied**) by foot soldiers (**Kernes**) and horsemen (**Gallowglasses**) from Ireland and the Hebrides (**the western isles**).

14–15 **And Fortune ...** *Fortune personified as a fickle prostitute on the side of the rebels, favouring Macdonwald's cause, then abandoning him.*

18 **smoked with ...** the sword steamed with the blood of those he had killed

19 **Like Valour's minion** *Macbeth is the special favourite of Courage (personified, like Fortune).*

22–23 **unseamed ...** tore him open from the navel (**nave**) to the jaw (**chaps** or chops).

30 **skipping** (1) lightly armed; (2) fleeing.

31 **surveying vantage** seeing his chance

32 **furbished** fresh

34–35 **Yes ...** *The captain is being heavily ironic.*

37 **overcharged ...** with double charges of gunpowder

40–41 **Except they meant ...** Unless they were intending to bathe in steaming blood or make the battlefield as memorable as (**memorise**) the scene of Christ's crucifixion (**Golgotha**).

And choke their art. The merciless Macdonwald
(Worthy to be a rebel, for to that   10
The multiplying villainies of nature
Do swarm upon him) from the western isles
Of Kernes and Gallowglasses is supplied;
And Fortune, on his damnèd quarrel smiling,
Showed like a rebel's whore: but all's too weak;   15
For brave Macbeth (well he deserves that name),
Disdaining Fortune, with his brandished steel,
Which smoked with bloody execution,
Like Valour's minion, carved out his passage,
Till he faced the slave;   20
Which ne'er shook hands, nor bade farewell to him,
Till he unseamed him from the nave to the chaps,
And fixed his head upon our battlements.

DUNCAN   O valiant cousin! worthy gentleman!

CAPTAIN   As whence the sun 'gins his reflection,   25
Shipwracking storms and direful thunders break,
So from that spring, whence comfort seemed to come,
Discomfort swells. Mark, King of Scotland, mark:
No sooner justice had, with valour armed,
Compelled these skipping Kernes to trust their
      heels,   30
But the Norweyan lord, surveying vantage,
With furbished arms, and new supplies of men,
Began a fresh assault.

DUNCAN   Dismayed not this
Our captains, Macbeth and Banquo?

CAPTAIN   Yes;
As sparrows eagles, or the hare the lion.   35
If I say sooth, I must report they were
As cannons overcharged with double cracks;
So they
Doubly redoubled strokes upon the foe:
Except they meant to bathe in reeking wounds,   40
Or memorise another Golgotha,
I cannot tell –
But I am faint; my gashes cry for help.

DUNCAN   So well thy words become thee, as thy wounds:

1.2 A camp near Forres

Rosse arrives and reports that Macbeth has defeated the Norwegians and taken the rebel Thane of Cawdor prisoner. Duncan sentences Cawdor to death and transfers his title to Macbeth.

Activities

Character review: Macbeth (1)

Shakespeare gives us a good deal of information about Macbeth before he actually appears.

1. List the expressions used of Macbeth which highlight his physical courage.
2. Discuss what we have learned about:
   - his position in the army
   - his family relationship to the King
   - people's opinions of his deeds in the recent battle
   - the reward coming to him.
3. Which of the facts learned about Macbeth seem to you to be the most important in helping to gain an impression of the man who is to be the central character in the story?

45 **smack of** are a sign of

46 **Thane** *the Scottish equivalent of 'Lord'*

47–48 **What a haste ...** By the look of him he is in a great hurry! He looks like someone who has extraordinary things to tell.

51–52 **... Norweyan banners flout ...** *It is an insult to have Norwegian flags flying over Scotland.*

53 **Norway himself** *Kings in Shakespeare are often called by the name of their country.*

53–60 Norway, with a huge army, and assisted by the Thane of Cawdor, began an ominous (**dismal**) battle, until Macbeth – heavily armoured (**lapped in proof**) as though newly married to **Bellona**, the Roman goddess of war – faced him with comparable courage and skill (**self-comparisons**) ... disciplining (**curbing**) his insolent (**lavish**) spirit, until finally we had victory.

62 **craves composition** is begging to discuss peace terms

64 **disbursèd** paid

64 **Saint Colmé's Inch** an island in the Firth of Forth

65 **dollars** *The dollar was first coined in the early sixteenth century.*

66–67 **... deceive Our bosom interest** deceive us in matters close to our heart

67 **present** immediate

They smack of honour both. – Go, get him
        surgeons.   45

Exit CAPTAIN, attended.

Enter ROSSE and ANGUS.

(*Turning*) Who comes here?

MALCOLM   The worthy Thane of Rosse.

LENOX   What a haste looks through his eyes!
                So should he look that seems to speak things strange.

ROSSE   God save the King!

DUNCAN   Whence camest thou, worthy thane?

ROSSE   From Fife, great King,   50
                Where the Norweyan banners flout the sky
                And fan our people cold.
                Norway himself, with terrible numbers,
                Assisted by that most disloyal traitor,
                The Thane of Cawdor, began a dismal conflict;   55
                Till that Bellona's bridegroom, lapped in proof,
                Confronted him with self-comparisons,
                Point against point, rebellious arm 'gainst arm,
                Curbing his lavish spirit: and, to conclude,
                The victory fell on us; –

DUNCAN   Great happiness!   60

ROSSE   That now
                Sweno, the Norways' king, craves composition;
                Nor would we deign him burial of his men
                Till he disbursèd at Saint Colmé's Inch
                Ten thousand dollars to our general use.   65

DUNCAN   No more that Thane of Cawdor shall deceive
                Our bosom interest. – Go, pronounce his present death,
                And with his former title greet Macbeth.

ROSSE   I'll see it done.

DUNCAN   What he hath lost, noble Macbeth hath won.   70

Exeunt.

1.3 A heath

The first witch relates how she will torment a sailor whose wife had been rude to her.

Activities

Character review: the Witches (1)

Discuss what you know about the spell that the Witches are planning against the sailor, and their reasons for doing it. What does it tell us about the ways in which they might treat Macbeth?

(A) Re-read lines 15–25 and discuss the rhythm of the Witches' verse: how many 'beats' are there per line? Compose your own Witches' curse, using the same rhyming couplets (pairs of lines which rhyme, such as 15–16) and rhythm as Shakespeare's Witches.

(B) Discuss the examples in this scene of the Witches' *malignity* (evil behaviour towards others).

(a) Grade their malign activities according to how serious you consider them to be; and

(b) discuss what possible motives might lie behind their actions.

For example, how serious is 'killing swine', and what reasons might the second Witch have had for doing it?

(C) Discuss what the effect is of opening the play, and then introducing the central character's first appearance, with the Witches. Which lines seem to you to be particularly significant in suggesting how the story and its themes might develop?

2 **Killing swine** *An animal's death would often be attributed to witches.*

5 **quoth** said

6 **Aroint thee** Get out of here!

rump-fed ronyon fat-bottomed hag

7 **the Tiger** *A ship called The Tiger returned from Aleppo (in Syria) after a terrifying voyage in 1606 lasting roughly* **sev'n-nights nine times nine** *(567 days – line 22).*

8–9 **in a sieve ...** *It was believed that witches could sail in sieves and turn themselves into animals (but that the tails would be missing).*

10 **I'll do ...** 'I'll do him!' *(do him mischief, cause him harm)*

14–17 **I myself have all the other ...** I have power over all the other winds, in every compass-point (**quarters ... I' the shipman's card**), *which prevent ships from getting safely into port.*

18 **I'll drain him dry** *because he won't be able to get into port to take on water*

20 **penthouse lid** his eyelid, *half-closed with sleep like the sloping roof of a lean-to shed*

21 **forbid** under a curse

23 **peak** become thin

24 **bark** ship

Scene 3

A heath.

Thunder. Enter THREE WITCHES.

1 WITCH	Where hast thou been, sister?
2 WITCH	Killing swine.
3 WITCH	Sister, where thou?
1 WITCH	A sailor's wife had chestnuts in her lap,

And munched, and munched, and munched: "Give
    me," quoth I: 5
"Aroint thee, witch!" the rump-fed ronyon cries.
Her husband's to Aleppo gone, master o' the Tiger:
But in a sieve I'll thither sail,
And, like a rat without a tail,
I'll do, I'll do, and I'll do.   10

2 WITCH	I'll give thee a wind.
1 WITCH	Th' art kind.
3 WITCH	And I another.
1 WITCH	I myself have all the other;

And the very ports they blow,   15
All the quarters that they know
I' the shipman's card;
I'll drain him dry as hay:
Sleep shall neither night nor day
Hang upon his penthouse lid;   20
He shall live a man forbid.
Weary sev'n-nights nine times nine,
Shall he dwindle, peak and pine:
Though his bark cannot be lost,
Yet it shall be tempest-tost.   25
Look what I have.

2 WITCH	Show me, show me.
1 WITCH	Here I have a pilot's thumb,

Wrecked, as homeward he did come.

1.3 A heath

The Witches greet Macbeth (who is Thane of Glamis) with the predictions that he will be Thane of Cawdor and King.

Activities

Shakespeare's language: antithesis

From the opening scene of the play, much of the characters' language is notable for its reference to opposites (or *antithesis* – plural: *antitheses*). For example:

- When the battle's *lost and won* (1.1.4)
- *Fair is foul*, and foul is fair (1.1.10)
- pronounce his *present* death, And with his *former* title greet Macbeth (1.2.67–68)
- What he hath *lost*, noble Macbeth hath *won* (1.2.70).

A As you read 1.3, find other examples of antithesis (those uttered by the Witches are extremely important) and discuss their meanings. Look at lines 51–52, 65, 66, 67, 81, 84–85, 131 and 141–142.

B Macbeth's first line in the play: 'So foul and fair a day I have not seen' (1.3.38) is an echo of one of the Witches' most powerful antitheses. Discuss what possible meanings the line might have.

C Discuss the effect of this repeated use of antithesis, for example the fact that Macbeth's first line is a repetition of the Witches' 'Fair is foul, and foul is fair'. (It has been said that it adds to the atmosphere of strangeness in the play; that it is unsettling; and that it makes it seem as though everyone is speaking in riddles.)

32 **weird** *from an Old English word meaning Fate*

33 **Posters** fast travellers

35 **thrice ...** *Three was thought to be a magic number; the witches might be dancing here.*

39 **is 't called** is it supposed to be

42–43 **are you aught ...?** Are you the kind of creatures that can answer questions?

44 **choppy** chapped, red and rough

45–46 **you should be women ...** You ought to be women, but your beards suggest otherwise.

50 **hereafter** at some time in the future

53–54 **Are ye fantastical ...?** Are you imaginary or as real as you seem to be?

55–57 **... with present grace ...** You greet him with his present title *(he is already Thane of Glamis)*, and also predict that he will have another noble title *(Thane of Cawdor)* and the hope of becoming king, so that he seems completely enthralled with it all.

Drum within

3 WITCH   A drum! a drum!   30
             Macbeth doth come.

ALL   The weird sisters, hand in hand,
             Posters of the sea and land,
             Thus do go about, about:
             Thrice to thine, and thrice to mine,   35
             And thrice again, to make up nine.
             Peace! – the charm's wound up.

Enter MACBETH and BANQUO.

MACBETH   So foul and fair a day I have not seen.

BANQUO   How far is 't called to Forres? – (*He notices the*
             WITCHES) What are these,
             So withered and so wild in their attire   40
             That look not like th' inhabitants o' the earth
             And yet are on 't? – (*He speaks to the WITCHES*) Live
             you? or are you aught
             That man may question? You seem to understand me,
             By each at once her choppy finger laying
             Upon her skinny lips: you should be women,   45
             And yet your beards forbid me to interpret
             That you are so.

MACBETH   Speak, if you can: – what are you?

1 WITCH   All hail, Macbeth! hail to thee, Thane of Glamis!

2 WITCH   All hail, Macbeth! hail to thee, Thane of Cawdor!

3 WITCH   All hail, Macbeth! that shalt be king hereafter.   50

BANQUO   (*Turning to MACBETH*) Good Sir, why do you start, and
             seem to fear
             Things that do sound so fair? – (*To the WITCHES*) I' the
             name of truth,
             Are ye fantastical, or that indeed
             Which outwardly ye show? My noble partner
             You greet with present grace, and great prediction   55
             Of noble having and of royal hope,
             That he seems rapt withal: to me you speak not.

1.3 A heath

Banquo asks the Witches to predict his future and they tell him that his descendants will be kings, though he himself will not.

Activities

Actors' interpretations (2): the Witches

How could you make the Witches 'vanish' (line 78) in a stage performance? (Look at what Macbeth and Banquo say in amazement: lines 79–85.) Discuss how their disappearance might be effected in the following performance spaces: (a) the floor of the school hall; (b) a modern professional theatre; (c) Shakespeare's Globe theatre; (d) a film; (e) any other staging of your choice.

The witches in 1986

58 look into the seeds of time predict the future

60–61 who neither beg nor fear ... who does not ask any favours of you, nor fear your hatred

67 get kings 'beget' kings, be the father of kings

70 imperfect incomplete *(because they seem to give only half the story)*

71 *According to the historian Holinshed, Macbeth inherited the title Thane of Glamis from his father, Sinel. (See the activity on page 189.) Modern historians believe that Macbeth reigned from 1040–1057 and that his father was Findleach. Both Macbeth and King Duncan were descendants of King Malcolm II; Macbeth was his nephew and Duncan his grandson.*

72 the Thane of Cawdor lives *Macbeth is not aware that Cawdor was treacherously assisting Norway (see line 108).*

73–75 and to be king ... The idea of becoming king is no more believable (**Stands not within the prospect of belief**) than the idea of being Thane of Cawdor.

77 blasted ravaged, battered by the weather

81 corporal flesh and blood, possessing a physical body

84–85 the insane root ... hemlock, *a drug which could cause madness*

	If you can look into the seeds of time,	
	And say which grain will grow, and which will not,	
	Speak then to me, who neither beg nor fear	60
	Your favours nor your hate.	

1 WITCH   Hail!

2 WITCH   Hail!

3 WITCH   Hail!

1 WITCH   Lesser than Macbeth, and greater.   65

2 WITCH   Not so happy, yet much happier.

3 WITCH   Thou shalt get kings, though thou be none:
So all hail, Macbeth and Banquo!

1 WITCH   Banquo and Macbeth, all hail!

MACBETH   Stay, you imperfect speakers, tell me more.   70
By Sinel's death, I know I am Thane of Glamis;
But how of Cawdor? the Thane of Cawdor lives,
A prosperous gentleman; and to be king
Stands not within the prospect of belief
No more than to be Cawdor. Say, from whence   75
You owe this strange intelligence? or why
Upon this blasted heath you stop our way
With such prophetic greeting? Speak, I charge you.

WITCHES vanish.

BANQUO   The earth hath bubbles, as the water has,
And these are of them. – Whither are they
       vanished?   80

MACBETH   Into the air; and what seemed corporal, melted
As breath into the wind. – Would they had stayed!

BANQUO   Were such things here, as we do speak about,
Or have we eaten on the insane root
That takes the reason prisoner?   85

MACBETH   Your children shall be kings.

BANQUO   *You* shall be king.

1.3　A heath

Rosse and Angus arrive to give the news that, as a reward for his bravery, Macbeth is to be made Thane of Cawdor.

Activities

Plot review (1): Rosse's news

Discuss the importance of the news that Rosse brings (lines 89–107).

(a) What does it show about Duncan's current opinion of Macbeth?

(b) What does it suggest about Macbeth's future under King Duncan?

(c) What effect might it have upon Macbeth himself, bearing in mind the Witches' prophecies?

Character review: Macbeth (2) and asides

Throughout Shakespeare's plays, characters will turn to the audience to voice thoughts which the other characters on stage do not hear. These are known as *asides*. Asides are vital in this scene in showing us how Macbeth reacts to the Witches' prophecies.

Ⓐ Read from line 109 to the end of the scene, picking out all the words which are spoken as asides. What kinds of things are going through Macbeth's head, that he is not willing to share with Banquo, Rosse and Angus?

(Continued on page 16)

90–93 and, when he reads . . . When the King reads about your own personal daring (**Thy personal venture**), he does not know whether to praise you or express his amazement.

93–97 Silenced with that . . . Speechless with admiration for that, he looks through the day's events and finds that you also fought against Norway, unafraid of the hideous scene of death and destruction that you yourself have created.

104 for an earnest as a pledge; a token 'down payment' of the greater reward to come

106 addition title

109 Who was the man who used to be

111–116 Whether he was . . . I don't know whether he was allied (**combined**) with the Norwegians, or strengthened them (**did line** – *as a lining strengthens a jacket*) by giving secret help and other advantages (**vantage**); or whether he worked to bring about his country's destruction (**wrack**) by doing both. But he has been destroyed by treacherous acts carrying the death penalty (**treasons capital**), which he has confessed and which have been proved against him.

1.3

MACBETH   And Thane of Cawdor too; went it not so?

BANQUO   To the selfsame tune and words. Who's here?

Enter ROSSE and ANGUS.

ROSSE   The king hath happily received, Macbeth,
            The news of thy success; and, when he reads   90
            Thy personal venture in the rebels' fight,
            His wonders and his praises do contend,
            Which should be thine, or his. Silenced with that,
            In viewing o'er the rest o' the selfsame day,
            He finds thee in the stout Norweyan ranks,   95
            Nothing afeard of what thyself didst make,
            Strange images of death. As thick as hail
            Ran post with post; and every one did bear
            Thy praises in his kingdom's great defence,
            And poured them down before him.

ANGUS   We are sent   100
            To give thee, from our royal master, thanks;
            Only to herald thee into his sight,
            Not pay thee.

ROSSE   And, for an earnest of a greater honour,
            He bade me, from him, call thee Thane of Cawdor: 105
            In which addition, Hail! most worthy thane,
            For it is thine.

BANQUO   What! can the devil speak true?

MACBETH   The Thane of Cawdor lives: why do you dress me
            In borrowed robes?

ANGUS   Who was the thane lives yet;
            But under heavy judgement bears that life   110
            Which he deserves to lose. Whether he was combined
            With those of Norway, or did line the rebel
            With hidden help and vantage, or that with both
            He laboured in his country's wrack, I know not;
            But treasons capital, confessed and proved,   115
            Have overthrown him.

MACBETH   (*Aside*) Glamis, and Thane of Cawdor:

1.3 A heath

Macbeth is amazed that the Witches' prediction has come true. Despite Banquo's warning that the Witches might be leading him to evil, Macbeth thinks about killing Duncan.

Activities

B To gain the full effect of how asides work, read from line 109 to the end of the scene in groups of three, with the actor playing Macbeth turning away very deliberately for each aside. Then rehearse the scene again more realistically, thinking carefully about what the other characters ought to be doing while Macbeth is speaking his asides to the audience.

C Discuss how the speeches, with their constant shifting from asides to 'public' utterances, help to establish what is happening to the relationship between Macbeth and Banquo.

1. What direction would you give to the actor playing Banquo concerning what he says to Rosse and Angus (line 127)?
2. How should the three be reacting while Macbeth is 'rapt' (127–142)?
3. How should Banquo deliver his comment about 'New honours' (144–146)? Should his tone be cheerful, for example? worried? matter-of-fact?
4. How should Banquo react to Macbeth's final words (153–156)? (Think, for example, about the variety of ways in which an actor can deliver 'Very gladly.')

117   **behind** yet to come

120–121   **That, trusted home ...** If you accepted that completely, it would inflame your hopes of becoming king.

123–126   **And oftentimes ...** Often, to lead us to destruction (**our harm**), agents of evil win our confidence by being honest about unimportant things (**trifles**), in order to deceive us when it really matters (**in deepest consequence**).

128–129   **As happy prologues ...** as promising introductions to the great theatrical experience (**swelling act**) of the story about becoming king (**imperial theme**)

132   **earnest of success** pledge that I will be successful

135   **unfix my hair** make my hair stand on end

137–138   **Present fears ...** Frightening things happening now are less terrifying than anything we can imagine.

139–142   **My thought ...** My thoughts, in which murder is so far only an idea (**fantastical**), disturb my body so much, that imagination makes me unable to act (**function is smothered in surmise**) and nothing seems real except the fantasy of being king.

144–145   **Like our strange garments** ... like new clothes which don't fit us properly (**cleave not to their mould**)

The greatest is behind. (*To* ROSSE *and* ANGUS) Thanks
   for your pains.
(*To* BANQUO) Do you not hope your children shall be
   kings,
When those that gave the Thane of Cawdor to me
Promised no less to them?

BANQUO   That, trusted home,   120
Might yet enkindle you unto the crown
Besides the Thane of Cawdor. But 't is strange:
And oftentimes, to win us to our harm,
The instruments of darkness tell us truths,
Win us with honest trifles, to betray 's   125
In deepest consequence. –
(*To* ROSSE *and* ANGUS) Cousins, a word, I pray you.

MACBETH   (*Aside*) Two truths are told
As happy prologues to the swelling act
Of the imperial theme. (*To* ROSSE *and* ANGUS) I thank
   you, gentlemen –
(*Aside*) This supernatural soliciting   130
Cannot be ill; cannot be good: – if ill,
Why hath it given me earnest of success,
Commencing in a truth? I am Thane of Cawdor:
If good, why do I yield to that suggestion
Whose horrid image doth unfix my hair,   135
And make my seated heart knock at my ribs
Against the use of nature? Present fears
Are less than horrible imaginings.
My thought, whose murder yet is but fantastical,
Shakes so my single state of man, that function   140
Is smothered in surmise, and nothing is,
But what is not.

BANQUO   (*To the lords*) Look, how our partner's rapt.

MACBETH   (*Aside*) If Chance will have me king, why, Chance may
   crown me,
Without my stir.

BANQUO   New honours come upon him
Like our strange garments, cleave not to their
   mould   145
But with the aid of use.

1.4 A room in the King's palace

Macbeth conceals his thoughts from Banquo. Duncan's son Malcolm reports that the rebel Cawdor had faced his execution with dignity.

Activities

Shakespeare's language: abbreviations

Shakespeare will often abbreviate phrases, sometimes to make the language sound natural (as we do in modern English with don't, I'll, we're, etc.); sometimes to get the right number of syllables into the line (see Shakespeare's verse, pages 201–204), and the result can be confusing in print.

1. Check that you understand the meanings of the following by finding them in the script and then, to get the pronunciation right, read out loud the complete line from which they come: 'Gainst (1.2.5); ne'er (1.2.21); 'gins (1.2.25); o' the (1.3.7); Th' art (1.3.12); I' the (1.3.17); is 't (1.3.39); th' inhabitants (1.3.41); on 't (1.3.42); o'er (1.3.94).

2. Discuss what effect these abbreviations have. Do they make the language sound more like everyday speech, for example?

Shakespeare's language: dramatic irony

Dramatic irony is a term used to describe a situation in which the audience knows something important that the character does not. Look again at lines 11–14 (including Macbeth's entrance and Duncan's greeting), and discuss this moment as an example of dramatic irony.

146–147 **Come what come may ...** Whatever happens, the roughest day will pass.

148 **we stay upon ...** we are ready to go if it suits you

149–150 **wrought With things forgotten** troubled by past events

150–152 **your pains ...** The troubles you have taken on my behalf are recorded in a book, and I read them each day, every time I turn a new page.

153–155 **Think about what hath chanced ...** Think over what has happened and, in due course, after we have thought it over in the meantime (**The interim having weighed it**), let's discuss it openly

Flourish fanfare

2 **in commission** who were given the job *(of executing Cawdor)*

6 **set forth** displayed

7–8 **Nothing in his life ...** Nothing in Cawdor's life showed his noble qualities (**Became him**) as clearly as his death did.

10 **owed** owned

11 **As 't were ...** as though it were something of no value

11–12 **There's no art ...** There is no skill which can teach you to discover people's thoughts (**the mind's construction**) by looking at their faces.

MACBETH   (*Aside*) Come what come may,
Time and the hour runs through the roughest day.

BANQUO   Worthy Macbeth, we stay upon your leisure.

MACBETH   (*To the lords*) Give me your favour: my dull brain was
          wrought
With things forgotten. Kind gentlemen, your pains   150
Are registered where every day I turn
The leaf to read them. – Let us toward the king. –
(*To* BANQUO) Think upon what hath chanced; and at
          more time,
The interim having weighed it, let us speak
Our free hearts each to other.

BANQUO   Very gladly.   155

MACBETH   Till then, enough. – (*To all*) Come, friends.

                                           Exeunt.

Scene 4

Forres. A room in the King's palace.

*Flourish of trumpets. Enter DUNCAN, MALCOLM, DONALBAIN,
LENOX and attendants.*

DUNCAN   Is execution done on Cawdor? Are not
Those in commission yet returned?

MALCOLM   My liege,
They are not yet come back; but I have spoke
With one that saw him die: who did report
That very frankly he confessed his treasons,   5
Implored your highness' pardon, and set forth
A deep repentance. Nothing in his life
Became him like the leaving it: he died
As one that had been studied in his death,
To throw away the dearest thing he owed   10
As 't were a careless trifle.

DUNCAN   There's no art
To find the mind's construction in the face:

1.4 A room in the King's palace

Duncan thanks Macbeth and Banquo for defeating the rebels and announces that his eldest son Malcolm will succeed him as king.

Activities

Actors' interpretations (3): naming Duncan's heir

When Laurence Olivier played Macbeth, he took the view that Macbeth himself had a strong claim to the throne: not only was his wife Duncan's niece, but he himself was the greatest general of his day. He therefore fully expected to be named as the next king (as the crown in those days was not necessarily handed down automatically to the king's eldest son). Following this interpretation, Olivier recalled that, when he entered in this scene (line 14), 'there was a coronet on the pillow; and as we came on, I looked at it and registered "Oh, already, fine ..." Then it goes to Duncan's son as Prince of Cumberland and it's a blow between the eyes.'

In groups of four or five, act out (a) Macbeth's entrance as Olivier interpreted it; and (b) the moment when Duncan shocks Macbeth by naming Malcolm as his heir, discussing first how Macbeth should react at this point (if indeed he should show any reaction at all).

16–18 **Thou art so far before ...** *Macbeth has performed so many exploits that Duncan cannot keep up with the rewards he owes him.*

18–20 **would thou hadst ...** I wish you had been less deserving, so that I might have been able to thank you and reward you in proportion to your merits.

21 **thy due** owing to you, what you deserve

23 **pays itself** carries its own reward

24–27 **our duties Are ...** Our duties are like children, who only do what they are supposed to do when they are protecting (**doing everything Safe toward**) your love and honour.

28–29 **I have begun to plant thee ...** *Duncan thinks of Macbeth as a tree which he will cultivate. There will be further rewards and promotion.*

31 **infold** embrace

33–35 **My plenteous joys ...** *Duncan is so happy that he weeps for joy.*

36 **nearest** closest in line to the throne

37–38 **establish our estate ...** settle the succession. *(Duncan publicly proclaims that his son Malcolm will be his heir.)*

39–42 *This title for Malcolm will not be the only honour given out; everybody who deserves an honour will receive one.*

1.4

He was a gentleman on whom I built
An absolute trust –

Enter MACBETH, BANQUO, ROSSE and ANGUS.

(*To* MACBETH) O worthiest cousin!
The sin of my ingratitude even now   15
Was heavy on me. Thou art so far before,
That swiftest wing of recompense is slow
To overtake thee: would thou hadst less deserved,
That the proportion both of thanks and payment
Might have been mine! only I have left to say: 20
More is thy due than more than all can pay.

MACBETH   The service and the loyalty I owe,
In doing it, pays itself. Your highness' part
Is to receive our duties: and our duties
Are to your throne and state, children and
        servants;   25
Which do but what they should, by doing everything
Safe toward your love and honour.

DUNCAN   Welcome hither:
I have begun to plant thee, and will labour
To make thee full of growing. (*To* BANQUO) – Noble
        Banquo,
That hast no less deserved, nor must be known   30
No less to have done so, let me infold thee,
And hold thee to my heart.

BANQUO   There if I grow,
The harvest is your own.

DUNCAN   My plenteous joys,
Wanton in fulness, seek to hide themselves
In drops of sorrow. – (*To all*) Sons, kinsmen,
        thanes,   35
And you whose places are the nearest, know,
We will establish our estate upon
Our eldest, Malcolm; whom we name hereafter
The Prince of Cumberland: which honour must
Not, unaccompanied, invest him only,   40
But signs of nobleness, like stars, shall shine

1.5 A room in Macbeth's castle

Macbeth is deeply unsettled by the naming of Malcolm as the next king. Lady Macbeth reads a letter from her husband which tells her about the Witches' prophecies.

Activities

Character review: Macbeth (3)

Re-read Macbeth's aside (48–53). Discuss what the following phrases suggest about the way his mind is working at this point:

- ... 'On which I must fall down, or else o'erleap': what might he mean by 'o'erleap'?
- What might his 'black and deep desires' be? And why should the stars have to hide their fires?
- He thinks about doing something which he will then be afraid to look at – 'Which the eye fears, when it is done, to see.' Predict what effect such a terrible deed might have upon him.

Character review: Macbeth (4)

Discuss the following important questions. There are no 'correct answers': make judgements based upon your response to the play so far and the evidence you can find in the script:

1. Have Macbeth and Lady Macbeth in the past discussed the possibility of Macbeth becoming king?
2. Do you feel that Macbeth has already decided that he has to kill Duncan?
3. What is Macbeth's view of the Witches? He says that '*they have*

(Continued on page 24)

43 **bind us further** increase our debt to you *(because Macbeth will now host Duncan in his castle)*

44 **The rest is labour ...** Anything not done on your behalf is hard work.

45 **harbinger** *officer sent ahead of the King to make arrangements*

52–53 **The eye wink at ...** Let my eyes keep shut (**wink**) and not see what my hand is doing, but let it be something which, when done, the eye will fear to look at.

54 **full so** so very

55 **And in his commendations I am fed** It is like food to me, to hear him praised.

58 **peerless** unmatchable, unrivalled

2 **the perfect'st report** the most reliable evidence

2–3 **mortal knowledge** the kind of knowledge that ordinary humans have

6 **missives** messengers

8 **coming-on of time** the future

9–10 **deliver thee** report to you

10–12 **that thou might'st not lose the dues of rejoicing ...** so that you don't miss out on the excitement of knowing what great things are in store for you

On all deservers – (*To* MACBETH) From hence to
   Inverness,
And bind us further to you.

MACBETH   The rest is labour, which is not used for you:
I'll be myself the harbinger, and make joyful   45
The hearing of my wife with your approach;
So, humbly take my leave.

DUNCAN   My worthy Cawdor!

MACBETH   (*Aside*) The Prince of Cumberland! – That is a step
On which I must fall down, or else o'erleap,
For in my way it lies. Stars, hide your fires!   50
Let not light see my black and deep desires;
The eye wink at the hand, yet let that be,
Which the eye fears, when it is done, to see.

Exit.

DUNCAN   True, worthy Banquo, he is full so valiant,
And in his commendations I am fed;   55
It is a banquet to me. Let's after him,
Whose care is gone before to bid us welcome:
It is a peerless kinsman.

Flourish. Exeunt.

Scene 5

Inverness. A room in Macbeth's castle.

Enter LADY MACBETH, reading a letter.

LADY
MACBETH   *"They met me in the day of success; and I have learnt by
the perfect'st report, they have more in them than mortal
knowledge. When I burned in desire to question them
further, they made themselves air, into which they
vanished. Whiles I stood rapt in the wonder of it, came   5
missives from the king, who all-hailed me 'Thane of
Cawdor'; by which title, before, these weird sisters
saluted me, and referred me to the coming-on of time,
with 'Hail, king that shalt be!' This have I thought
good to deliver thee, my dearest partner of greatness,   10*

1.5   A room in Macbeth's castle

Lady Macbeth reflects that her husband has too much natural goodness in him to kill Duncan, but is delighted to hear the news that the King will be staying in their castle that very night.

Activities

more in them than mortal knowledge' (1.5.2–3), but how far does he trust them?

A Lady Macbeth's comments about her husband's character are expressed in complex language. In pairs, discuss each of her opinions (starting with 'Yet I do fear thy nature . . .') using the notes as a guide, to make sure that you have understood what she thinks of him.

B Write the opening paragraphs of Macbeth's letter, in which he tells his wife about the manner in which he happened to meet the Witches, and relates his reactions to their prophecies and his thoughts about Banquo. Then, imagining that you are Lady Macbeth, write comments in the margin of the letter, using phrases from her observations in lines 16–25.

B Look closely at Lady Macbeth's opinions on her husband's character (lines 16–25).
1. Discuss whether you think they are a fair assessment of Macbeth's character from what we have seen of him so far (her opinion might be one-sided and unfair).
2. Assuming her character analysis to be accurate, predict what it should prepare us for in terms of (a) the relationship between Macbeth and Lady Macbeth; and (b) future events.

16   **the milk of human kindness** *. . . the natural qualities that Macbeth inherited from his mother, of behaving like a decent human being.*

17   **catch . . .** take the quick route

     wouldst be would like to be

19   **illness** evil

     attend accompany

19–21   Anything you really want (**wouldst highly**), you want to achieve by fair means (**holily**); you don't want to cheat (**play false**), but would be quite happy to win unfairly.

23–24   while you want the murder done, you're afraid to do it yourself.

24   **Hie thee hither** hurry here

25–29   **pour my spirits . . .** So that I can influence you with evil thoughts and argue away (**chastise . . . tongue**) everything that stands in the way of the crown (**the golden round**), which fate and supernatural help seem to have crowned you with already.

34   **had the speed of** overtook

36   **Give him tending** look after him

37   **The raven** *Ravens were the messengers of death.*

39–40   **spirits That tend on mortal thoughts** evil spirits which listen to murderous plans

that thou might'st not lose the dues of rejoicing, by being
ignorant of what greatness is promised thee. Lay it to thy
heart, and farewell."

Glamis thou art, and Cawdor; and shalt be
What thou art promised. – Yet do I fear thy nature: 15
It is too full o' the milk of human kindness
To catch the nearest way. Thou wouldst be great;
Art not without ambition, but without
The illness should attend it: what thou wouldst
   highly,
That wouldst thou holily; wouldst not play false,   20
And yet wouldst wrongly win; thou 'dst have, great
   Glamis,
That which cries, "Thus thou must do, if thou have
   it";
And that which rather thou dost fear to do,
Than wishest should be undone. Hie thee hither,
That I may pour my spirits in thine ear,   25
And chastise with the valour of my tongue
All that impedes thee from the golden round,
Which fate and metaphysical aid doth seem
To have thee crowned withal. –

Enter a MESSENGER.

                              What is your tidings?

MESSENGER   The king comes here tonight.

LADY   Thou 'rt mad to say it.   30
MACBETH   Is not thy master with him? who, were 't so,
Would have informed for preparation.

MESSENGER   So please you, it is true: our thane is coming;
One of my fellows had the speed of him,
Who, almost dead for breath, had scarcely more   35
Than would make up his message.

LADY   Give him tending:
MACBETH   He brings great news. (*Exit MESSENGER*) The raven
   himself is hoarse
That croaks the fatal entrance of Duncan
Under my battlements. Come, you spirits

1.5 A room in Macbeth's castle

Lady Macbeth calls upon evil spirits to assist her. When Macbeth arrives, she tells him to look innocent and leave everything to her.

Activities

Character review: Lady Macbeth (1) and soliloquies

A soliloquy is a speech in which the character speaks their thoughts to the audience. In these two soliloquies, Lady Macbeth reveals her reactions to a letter from her husband in which he tells her about the meeting with the Witches (1–29), and then prepares herself for what has to be done (37–53). Work in pairs to express her thoughts in your own words, using the following as a structure:

The Witches have prophesied that you will be king, but you worry me:

- 15–17 Yet ... way   ...
- 17–19 Thou ... attend it   ...
- 19–20 what ... holily   ...
- 20–21 wouldst ... win   ...
- 21–24 thou'dst ... undone   ...

Get here quickly, so that I can work on you:

- 24–25 Hie thee ... ear   ...
- 26–29 And chastise ... withal   ...

Duncan's arrival here will be fatal to him:

- 37–39 The raven ... battlements ...

I must turn myself into a pitiless creature:

- 39–42 Come ... cruelty!   ...
- 42–46 make thick ... and it!   ...
- 46–49 Come to ... mischief!   ...
- 49–53 Come, thick ... hold!   ...

40 **unsex me here** remove all my feminine qualities

44–46 **That no compunctious visitings ...** So that no pangs of conscience get in the way of my deadly intentions (**fell purpose**), nor come between my plan and the execution of it (**Th' effect and it**).

47–49 **take my milk for gall** Take away my milk and put bitter poison in its place, you spirits (**ministers**) of murder, wherever, in your invisible bodies (**sightless substances**), you serve (**wait on**) the evil in nature!

50 **pall thee ...** shroud yourself *(like the covering for a corpse)* in the darkest (**dunnest**) smoke from hell

53 **Hold** stop

55–57 **Thy letters ...** Your letters have transported me in my imagination so that the future seems to be happening now.

59 **as he purposes** so he intends

62–64 **To beguile the time, Look like the time ...** To deceive the world, look as people expect you to look: be welcoming in your appearance, behaviour and speech (**eye...hand...tongue**).

66 **provided for** (1) looked after; (2) dealt with

67 **despatch** management

69 **solely sovereign sway** the absolute power of the throne

That tend on mortal thoughts, unsex me here,   40
And fill me, from the crown to the toe, top-full
Of direst cruelty! make thick my blood,
Stop up th' access and passage to remorse;
That no compunctious visitings of nature
Shake my fell purpose, nor keep peace between   45
Th' effect and it! Come to my woman's breasts,
And take my milk for gall, you murdering
     ministers,
Wherever in your sightless substances
You wait on nature's mischief! Come, thick night,
And pall thee in the dunnest smoke of hell,   50
That my keen knife see not the wound it makes,
Nor heaven peep through the blanket of the dark
To cry, "Hold, hold!"

Enter MACBETH.

             Great Glamis! worthy Cawdor!
Greater than both, by the all-hail, hereafter!
Thy letters have transported me beyond   55
This ignorant present, and I feel now
The future in the instant.

MACBETH   My dearest love,
Duncan comes here tonight.

LADY
MACBETH   And when goes hence?

MACBETH   Tomorrow, as he purposes.

LADY   O! never
MACBETH   Shall sun that morrow see!   60
Your face, my thane, is as a book, where men
May read strange matters. To beguile the time,
Look like the time, bear welcome in your eye,
Your hand, your tongue: look like the innocent
     flower
But be the serpent under 't. He that's coming   65
Must be provided for; and you shall put
This night's great business into my despatch;
Which shall to all our nights and days to come
Give solely sovereign sway and masterdom.

1.6 Outside Macbeth's castle

Duncan arrives, admires the beautiful setting of Macbeth's castle and is welcomed by Lady Macbeth.

Activities

Actors' interpretations (4)

A Draw three or four frames of a storyboard for a film version, focusing on the opening moments of scene 6 before any of the dialogue has been spoken. The shots should show the scenery and the castle architecture. Add notes around each frame, showing how the scene reflects particular observations made by Duncan and Banquo in lines 1–10. (You might, for example, show the 'temple–haunting martlet' and put a note to that effect.)

B Make a list of all the references in scene 6 which emphasise that (a) Macbeth's castle is a beautiful place; and that (b) Duncan is receiving a hearty welcome. For each one, pick out a statement by Lady Macbeth in scene 5 which shows that (a) her intentions are evil; and (b) the welcome will be false and hypocritical.

C Sinéad Cusack described her entrance at line 10 like this:

'All those rough soldiers were lying around, and then this woman swept through them in a green dress and red shawl. To those men she was like a vision, a drink of water in the desert.

(Continued on page 30)

70–71 **Only look up clear** ... Just maintain an innocent face: constantly changing your expression is a sign of fear.

Hautboys oboes *(French: hautbois)*

1 **seat** setting, situation

1–3 **the air Nimbly** ... The air is eager to come forward and show its qualities to our senses.

4–6 **temple-haunting martlet** ... The house martin, which often builds its nest in churches, proves (**does approve**), by making it its favourite abode (**loved mansionry**), that the heavenly breeze has an alluring scent here.

6–8 There is no piece of projecting building (**jutty** ...) or convenient corner (**coign of vantage**) in which the martin has not built a hanging (**pendent**) nest and cradle for its young.

11–14 The love shown to me is sometimes a nuisance, but I am always (**still**) grateful because it *is* love. In this way I am teaching you how to ask God to reward (**yield**) me for the trouble you are taking, and thank me for inflicting it upon you.

18 **for those of old** ... For the honours given in the past (**those of old**) and the ones added recently (**late**), we will – like hermits – always pray for you,

1.6

MACBETH	We will speak further.

LADY
MACBETH
        Only look up clear;   **70**
To alter favour ever is to fear.
Leave all the rest to me.

Exeunt.

Scene 6

The same. Before the castle. Hautboys and torches.

Enter DUNCAN, MALCOLM, DONALBAIN, BANQUO, LENOX,
MACDUFF, ROSSE, ANGUS and attendants.

DUNCAN This castle hath a pleasant seat; the air
Nimbly and sweetly recommends itself
Unto our gentle senses.

BANQUO   This guest of summer,
The temple-haunting martlet, does approve,
By his loved mansionry, that the heaven's breath **5**
Smells wooingly here: no jutty, frieze,
Buttress, nor coign of vantage, but this bird
Hath made his pendent bed, and procreant cradle:
Where they most breed and haunt, I have observed,
The air is delicate.

Enter LADY MACBETH.

DUNCAN   See, see! our honoured hostess. – **10**
(*To* LADY MACBETH) The love that follows us sometime
  is our trouble,
Which still we thank as love. Herein I teach you,
How you shall bid God yield us for your pains,
And thank us for your trouble.

LADY
MACBETH
          All our service,
In every point twice done, and then done double, **15**
Were poor and single business to contend
Against those honours deep and broad, wherewith
Your majesty loads our house: for those of old,
And the late dignities heaped up to them,
We rest your hermits.

29

A room in Macbeth's castle

Lady Macbeth leads Duncan into the castle. Macbeth is deeply troubled by the possible consequences of killing the King and considers the powerful reasons against the deed.

Activities

I felt very strongly that the scene had to be beautiful, and she had to look welcoming, to highlight the horror of what she was doing – and all those men had to react to her.'

Act out the whole scene, following Sinéad Cusack's interpretation, and discuss its success. In particular, what is the effect of playing Lady Macbeth as though she is a genuinely welcoming hostess? Discuss other ways in which the scene might be interpreted on stage.

Shakespeare's language: euphemism

Macbeth's and Lady Macbeth's language is full not only of ambiguity (see page 39) but also of *euphemism*: words and expressions that are used to cover up unpleasant ideas (as, for example, when someone is said to have 'passed away' rather than 'died'). As you read through Macbeth's soliloquy (lines 1–28), list all the different ways in which he avoids actually saying 'the murder' (such as 'it' in line 1). There are examples in lines 1, 2, 4 (two examples), 7, 9, 11, 14, 16, 20, 24, 26. What does this heavy use of euphemism suggest about Macbeth's state of mind?

21 **coursed him at the heels** chased closely behind him

22 **purveyor** *the official who rode ahead of the king*

25–28 **Your servants ...** Everything that we (**Your servants**) own, is held in trust (**in compt**) for you; and we will give an account (**audit**) whenever you want one, and always (**Still**) return everything to you.

   sewer *the chief servant*

   divers *various*

1 **If it were done ...** If the killing would be the end of the business

2–7 If the assassination could prevent (**trammel**) any further trouble, and achieve success (**catch ... success**) with Duncan's death (**his surcease**); so that this single blow might be all that's needed (**the be-all ...**) here on earth (**this bank ... time**), I'd risk punishment in the afterlife.

7–8 **But, in these cases ...** but for crimes like this we always (**still**) receive sentence on earth (**have judgement here**)

8–10 **that we but teach ...** because we give lessons in violence (**Bloody instructions**) and it is then used against us

11–12 **Commends th' ingredients ...** makes us drink our own poison

12 **He's here ...** There are two reasons why Duncan should trust me.

| DUNCAN | Where's the Thane of Cawdor? | 20 |

                    We coursed him at the heels, and had a purpose
To be his purveyor: but he rides well;
And his great love, sharp as his spur, hath holp him
To his home before us. Fair and noble hostess,
We are your guest tonight.

LADY
MACBETH   Your servants ever   25
Have theirs, themselves, and what is theirs, in
    compt,
To make their audit at your highness' pleasure,
Still to return your own.

DUNCAN   Give me your hand;
Conduct me to mine host: we love him highly,
And shall continue our graces towards him.   30
By your leave, hostess.

                                     Exeunt.

Scene 7

The same. A room in the castle. Hautboys and torches.

Enter, and pass over the stage, a sewer, and divers servants with dishes and service. Then enter MACBETH.

MACBETH   (*Aside*) If it were done when 't is done, then 't were
    well
It were done quickly: if the assassination
Could trammel up the consequence, and catch
With his surcease success; that but this blow
Might be the be-all and the end-all here,   5
But here upon this bank and shoal of time,
We'd jump the life to come. – But, in these cases,
We still have judgement here, that we but teach
Bloody instructions, which, being taught, return
To plague th' inventor: this even-handed justice   10
Commends th' ingredients of our poisoned chalice
To our own lips. He's here in double trust:
First, as I am his kinsman and his subject,
Strong both against the deed; then, as his host,
Who should against his murderer shut the door,   15

1.7 A room in Macbeth's castle

Macbeth thinks about Duncan's virtues and imagines the terrible reactions to his murder. When he tells his wife that they must not proceed with their plans to kill Duncan, she accuses him of cowardice.

Activities

Character review: Macbeth (5)

This is one of the most revealing soliloquies in the play (lines 1–28). In order to gain a deeper understanding of what is going on in Macbeth's head, work in pairs to express the main points of his argument in your own words, using the following as a structure:

It would be all right if:
- 1–2 . . .
- 2–4 . . .
- 4–7 . . .

But it's not like that; the problem is:
- 7–10 . . .
- 10–12 . . .

And here are the reasons why I should not kill him:
- 12–16 (a) . . .
- (b) . . .
- 16–20 . . .
- 21–25 . . .
- 25–28 . . .

17–18 borne his faculties ... Duncan has used his powers as a king so humbly (**meek**) and has been such a perfect (**clear**) ruler that

20 taking-off murder

21–25 And pity ... *Macbeth personifies pity as an innocent baby standing astride the tempest (**blast**) of fury which would arise after Duncan's murder; and then as a child-angel (**cherubin**) riding the winds (**sightless couriers of the air**), blowing the horror of the murder into people's eyes to make them weep.*

25–28 I have no spur ... *Macbeth's only incentive is ambition, which is like a rider who tries to vault into the saddle, but jumps too far and falls on the other side.*

35–39 Was the hope drunk...? Were you so optimistic earlier simply because you were drunk? Have you now woken, as though after a hangover, and feel sick (**green and pale**) about it all? From now on I will regard your love as drunken lechery too.

39–41 Art thou afeard...? Are you afraid to match your desires with actions?

42 esteem'st consider to be

44 Letting "I dare not" ... not daring to do what you really want to do

45 adage proverb (*'The cat wanted to eat fish, but didn't want to wet her paws.'*)

Not bear the knife myself. Besides, this Duncan
Hath borne his faculties so meek, hath been
So clear in his great office, that his virtues
Will plead like angels, trumpet-tongued, against
The deep damnation of his taking-off;   20
And pity, like a naked new-born babe,
Striding the blast, or heaven's cherubin, horsed
Upon the sightless couriers of the air,
Shall blow the horrid deed in every eye,
That tears shall drown the wind. – I have no spur   25
To prick the sides of my intent, but only
Vaulting ambition, which o'erleaps itself
And falls on the other –

Enter LADY MACBETH.

How now! what news?

LADY MACBETH	He has almost supped. Why have you left the chamber?
MACBETH	Hath he asked for me?
LADY MACBETH	Know you not he has? 30

MACBETH We will proceed no further in this business:
He hath honoured me of late; and I have bought
Golden opinions from all sorts of people,
Which would be worn now in their newest gloss,
Not cast aside so soon.

LADY
MACBETH   Was the hope drunk,   35
Wherein you dressed yourself? hath it slept since,
And wakes it now, to look so green and pale
At what it did so freely? From this time
Such I account thy love. Art thou afeard
To be the same in thine own act and valour,   40
As thou art in desire? Wouldst thou have that
Which thou esteem'st the ornament of life,
And live a coward in thine own esteem,
Letting "I dare not" wait upon "I would,"
Like the poor cat i' the adage?

1.7 A room in Macbeth's castle

Lady Macbeth declares that she would kill her own baby rather than break a promise as Macbeth had done, and explains her plans for blaming Duncan's murder on his bodyguards.

Activities

Actors' interpretations (5)

It is possible to interpret Shakespeare's plays in many different ways.

1. In pairs, see how many different ways you can act out lines 59–61: 'If we should fail . . . not fail.'
2. Discuss the different meanings that you have discovered. Bear in mind that:
   - there could be a different punctuation mark after Lady Macbeth's 'We fail' (e.g. an exclamation mark)
   - 'but' in Shakespeare's language can often mean 'only' or 'just'.
3. Bearing in mind what you know about these characters, discuss which meaning you think fits best.

Character review: Lady Macbeth (2)

A Lady Macbeth uses a number of methods to persuade her husband to go through with the murder. Find lines which mean something like:
- Were you drunk when you suggested the murder to me?
- You will do this if you love me.
- Are you afraid to get what you want?
- You're not a real man if you don't do this.

(Continued on page 36)

45 **Pr'ythee** I beg you, 'I pray thee'

46 **may become** is fitting for

47 **none** subhuman

48 **break** reveal

50–51 **And, to be more . . .** And to behave even more bravely than you did then, would make you even more of a man.

51–54 **Nor time nor place . . .** Neither the time nor the place were right then (**Did then adhere**), and yet you were prepared to make them right; now the circumstances *are* right, you have lost your courage.

60 **But screw your courage . . .** *This image could refer either to the crossbow (which had a notch –* **sticking place** *– that the string had to be screwed up to), or to a musical instrument in which the string had to be tightened to the right point.*

62–63 **Whereto the rather . . .** and he is more likely to sleep soundly after his hard journey

63–67 **his two . . .** I will so overcome (**convince**) his two attendants (**chamberlains**) with wine and strong drink (**wassail**), that their memory, the guardian (**warder**) of the brain, will become foggy (**a fume**), and the brain itself, holder of reason, a mere chemist's flask for holding impure liquids (**limbeck**).

70 **put upon** blame on

71 **spongy** drink-sodden

72 **quell** murder

MACBETH	Pr'ythee, peace. 45
	I dare do all that may become a man;
	Who dares do more is none.
LADY	What beast was 't then
MACBETH	That made you break this enterprise to me?
	When you durst do it, then you were a man;
	And, to be more than what you were, you would 50
	Be so much more the man. Nor time nor place
	Did then adhere, and yet you would make both:
	They have made themselves, and that their fitness
	now
	Does unmake you. I have given suck, and know
	How tender 't is to love the babe that milks me: 55
	I would, while it was smiling in my face,
	Have plucked my nipple from his boneless gums,
	And dashed the brains out, had I so sworn as you
	Have done to this.
MACBETH	If we should fail, –
LADY	We fail?
MACBETH	But screw your courage to the sticking-place 60
	And we'll not fail. When Duncan is asleep
	(Whereto the rather shall his day's hard journey
	Soundly invite him), his two chamberlains
	Will I with wine and wassail so convince,
	That memory, the warder of the brain, 65
	Shall be a fume, and the receipt of reason
	A limbeck only: when in swinish sleep
	Their drenchèd natures lie, as in a death,
	What cannot you and I perform upon
	Th' unguarded Duncan? What not put upon 70
	His spongy officers, who shall bear the guilt
	Of our great quell?
MACBETH	Bring forth men-children only!
	For thy undaunted mettle should compose
	Nothing but males. Will it not be received,
	When we have marked with blood those sleepy
	two 75
	Of his own chamber, and used their very daggers,
	That they have done 't?

1.7 A room in Macbeth's castle

Convinced by his wife's words, Macbeth agrees to her plan and says that in the meantime they must both appear innocent and welcoming.

Activities

- If I had sworn to do something I would go through with it, however terrible it was.
- If you keep your courage up, we will succeed.
- This is what we will do . . .
- Nobody will dare challenge our interpretation of events, once Duncan is dead.

B In pairs, improvise 1.7.28–61, bringing out, in your own words, the ways in which Lady Macbeth manages to persuade her husband.

C After weighing up the reasons for and against killing Duncan, Macbeth says 'We will proceed no further in this business' (31), and yet, by the end of scene 7 (82), he has had his mind changed. Write a brief account of the ways in which Lady Macbeth persuades him, including: (a) references to the following key words and phrases: 'green and pale' (37), 'thy love' (39), 'afeard' (39), 'coward' (43), '"I dare not"' (44), '. . . durst . . . man' (49), 'more the man' (51), and her statement beginning 'I have given suck . . .' (54–59); and (b) comments on her proposed plans (line 61 onwards).

77 **other** in any other way

78–79 **As we shall . . .** because we will express so much grief and show our fury at his death

79–80 **bend up . . .** prepare *(like bending a bow)* all the strength in my body (**Each corporal agent**)

81 **mock the time . . .** deceive everybody by appearing virtuous

LADY   Who dares receive it other,
MACBETH   As we shall make our griefs and clamour roar
          Upon his death?

MACBETH   I am settled, and bend up
          Each corporal agent to this terrible feat.   80
          Away, and mock the time with fairest show:
          False face must hide what the false heart doth know.

                                                            Exeunt.

Exam practice

Character review: Macbeth (6)

Write the formal document in which King Duncan confers on Macbeth the title of Thane of Cawdor. Include lists of:
- all the great things that Macbeth has done, especially in the recent battle
- Macbeth's strengths and virtues, as Duncan sees them.

You might begin: 'Duncan, by the grace of God King of the Scots, to all his thanes sends greetings. Know that we have conferred the title of Thane of Cawdor on our dearly beloved cousin Macbeth . . .'

A Make notes on the most important things that you have learned about Macbeth in Act 1. Include:
- his success as a general
- other people's views of him
- his attitude to the Witches
- his ambitions to be king
- his relationship with his wife
- his feelings about killing Duncan.

B Imagine you are Macbeth. Write down your thoughts as you return to the banqueting chamber at the end of scene 7. You could begin: 'Despite all doubts, my mind is made up . . .'

Before you begin to write, you should work out how Macbeth might feel about:
- the possibility of being punished for murdering the King (either during his life or in the afterlife)
- the reasons against killing such a good king as Duncan
- the ways in which Lady Macbeth persuaded him
- the murder plan that she has suggested to him.

C Write an account of your personal responses to the character of Macbeth, as it has been presented in Act 1. Refer to other people's views of him (e.g. after the battle), his responses to the Witches, his feelings about the crown and the question of Duncan's murder, and his relationship with his wife. How do *you* respond to the character at this stage in the play? What are his strengths and weaknesses, for example? What can you admire in him and what troubles you about his character?

Character review: Banquo (1)

Write the letter that Banquo sends to his wife, similar to the one Macbeth sends to Lady Macbeth after meeting the Witches. Think about:
- the view he takes of the Witches' prophecies (look especially at 1.3.120–126)
- his opinion of the way in which Macbeth seemed to react, especially after Rosse brought news that Macbeth had been made Thane of Cawdor (1.3.142, 144–146)
- his thoughts about what might happen next.

Shakespeare's language: ambiguity

When a statement can have more than one meaning, we say that it is ambiguous and talk about *ambiguity*. Discuss the ambiguity in the following lines from Act 1, Scene 5 and consider what advice you would give to the actors playing Macbeth and Lady Macbeth on how to say them:
- Tomorrow, as he purposes (1.5.59)
- He that's coming Must be provided for (1.5.65–66)
- and you shall put This night's great business into my dispatch (1.5.66–67)
- Leave all the rest to me (1.5.72)

Three of these statements are spoken by Lady Macbeth. What does it tell you about her, if she utters so many ambiguous statements?

Themes: appearance and reality

A theme is a subject which is followed through the play and looked at from different angles. One of Shakespeare's commonest themes is concerned with the fact that things are frequently not what they seem: appearances can be deceptive. We can call this the theme of *Appearance and Reality*.

1. Discuss the meanings of the following statements:
   - Good Sir, why do you start and seem to fear
     Things that do sound so fair? (1.3.51–52)

   - Are ye fantastical, or that indeed
     Which outwardly ye show? (1.3.53–54)

   -       There's no art
     To find the mind's construction in the face:
     He was a gentleman on whom I built
     An absolute trust – (1.4.11–14)

   -       To beguile the time,
     Look like the time, bear welcome in your eye,
     Your hand, your tongue: look like the innocent flower
     But be the serpent under 't. (1.5.62–65)

2. In what ways does each one deal with the idea that appearances can be deceptive?
3. Discuss why you think this theme might have interested Shakespeare so much: think about his daily working life, for example.
4. What evidence is there in the world around us to support this idea that appearances can be deceptive? (Think not only about people but the natural world generally.)
5. In what ways is this theme particularly fitting for the story of Macbeth and his dealings with (a) the Witches; and (b) the people around him?

A courtyard within Macbeth's castle

Troubled by his thoughts, Banquo is unable to sleep. Meeting Macbeth, he tells him of Duncan's gratitude for the hospitality he has received and they begin to talk about the Witches.

Activities

Shakespeare's language: the royal plural (1)

Kings and queens tend to use 'we' and 'our', rather than 'I' and 'my'. This usage is known as the 'royal plural'. Re-read Macbeth's conversation with Banquo (lines 10–30) and note the number of times Macbeth refers to himself (a) in the plural, and (b) in the more usual singular. Discuss what this mixture might reveal about Macbeth's state of mind (taking account of the contexts in which he uses the different forms) and about his self-image at this point.

Character review: Banquo (2)

A There is some contrast between Banquo and Macbeth in Banquo's brief appearance in this scene. Discuss the lines which show (a) Banquo to be a virtuous man, clearly worried by something; and (b) Macbeth to be a treacherous schemer.

B Hot-seat Banquo and ask him, among other questions, what his reaction was to this conversation with Macbeth.

C Write Banquo's diary entry for this particular day, in which he comments to himself on this odd conversation with Macbeth and thinks about it in the light of Macbeth's reactions to the Witches' prophecies.

2 **is down** has set

4–5 **husbandry . . .** good housekeeping *(they are saving on candles)*

6–9 **A heavy summons . . .** I am desperate to sleep, but I can't; I wish the angels (**merciful powers**) could keep back the terrible thoughts that come to me when I am asleep.

13–17 **. . . in unusual pleasure . . .** He has had a particularly enjoyable time and has sent magnificent gifts (**largess**) to your servants' quarters (**offices**). He greets your wife with (**withal**) this diamond and has gone to bed (*or*: finished his speech – **shut up**) extremely happy.

17–19 **Being unprepared . . .** As we were not prepared for his visit, we could not be as generous (**free**) (in our hospitality) as we would have liked.

22 **entreat an hour to serve** find a convenient time

Act 2

Scene 1

The same. A court within the castle.

Enter BANQUO and FLEANCE with a torch before him.

BANQUO   How goes the night, boy?

FLEANCE   The moon is down; I have not heard the clock.

BANQUO   And she goes down at twelve.

FLEANCE   I take 't, 't is later, Sir.

BANQUO   Hold, take my sword. – There's husbandry in heaven;
Their candles are all out. – Take thee that, too.   **5**
A heavy summons lies like lead upon me,
And yet I would not sleep: merciful powers!
Restrain in me the cursèd thoughts that nature
Gives way to in repose! – Give me my sword.

Enter MACBETH, and a servant with a torch.

(*To MACBETH*) Who's there?   **10**

MACBETH   A friend.

BANQUO   What, Sir! not yet at rest? The king's a-bed:
He hath been in unusual pleasure, and
Sent forth great largess to your offices.
This diamond he greets your wife withal,   **15**
By the name of most kind hostess, and shut up
In measureless content.

MACBETH   Being unprepared,
Our will became the servant to defect,
Which else should free have wrought.

BANQUO   All's well.
I dreamt last night of the three weird sisters: **20**
To you they have showed some truth.

MACBETH   I think not of them:
Yet, when we can entreat an hour to serve,
We would spend it in some words upon that business,

2.1 A courtyard within Macbeth's castle

Making it very clear that he is loyal to Duncan, Banquo leaves Macbeth alone. Suddenly Macbeth has a vision of a blood-stained dagger.

Activities

Character review: Macbeth (7)

A Imagine a film version of Macbeth's soliloquy. Do a rough sketch of five frames of a storyboard, bringing out the nightmarish quality of his experience, writing the appropriate lines from the speech under each frame. You could choose to illustrate lines 33–34, 42, 46, 49–50, 52–54.

Ian McKellan as Macbeth in 1976

(Continued on page 44)

26–29 **So I lose none ...** So long as I don't lose honour by attempting to add honours to (**augment**) it, but always (**still**) keep my conscience clear (**bosom franchised**) and my loyalty to the King unblemished (**allegiance clear**), I am happy to accept advice (**be counselled**). *(Banquo seems to be telling Macbeth he will join his side only if there is to be no foul play).*

32 **She strike upon the bell** *This is to be the signal for killing Duncan.*

39 **heat-oppressèd** feverish

44–45 **Mine eyes ...** Either my eyes are stupid compared to all the other senses, or else they are more believable than all the rest.

46 **dudgeon** hilt, handle

48–49 **It is the bloody business ...** The violence of the act is making me see physical shapes in this way (**informs Thus to mine eyes**).

52 **Hecate** *the goddess of witchcraft*

52–56 **withered Murder ...** *Murder is imagined as a withered figure, called into action (**Alarumed**) by the howl of his sentry (**sentinel**) the wolf, stealthily striding towards his purpose (**design**), as the Roman Tarquin did on his way to rape (**ravishing**) Lucretia.*

If you would grant the time.

BANQUO   At your kind'st leisure.

MACBETH   If you shall cleave to my consent, when 't is,   25
It shall make honour for you.

BANQUO   So I lose none
In seeking to augment it, but still keep
My bosom franchised, and allegiance clear,
I shall be counselled.

MACBETH   Good repose the while!

BANQUO   Thanks, Sir: the like to you.   30

Exeunt BANQUO and FLEANCE.

MACBETH   (*To the servant*) Go, bid thy mistress, when my drink
    is ready,
She strike upon the bell. Get thee to bed. –

Exit servant.

Is this a dagger which I see before me,
The handle toward my hand? (*He speaks to the dagger*)
    Come, let me clutch thee: –
I have thee not, and yet I see thee still.   35
Art thou not, fatal vision, sensible
To feeling as to sight? or art thou but
A dagger of the mind, a false creation,
Proceeding from the heat-oppressèd brain?
I see thee yet, in form as palpable   40
As this which now I draw.
Thou marshall'st me the way that I was going;
And such an instrument I was to use. –
Mine eyes are made the fools o' the other senses,
Or else worth all the rest: I see thee still;   45
And on thy blade and dudgeon gouts of blood,
Which was not so before. – There's no such thing.
It is the bloody business which informs
Thus to mine eyes. – Now o'er the one half world
Nature seems dead, and wicked dreams abuse   50
The curtained sleep: witchcraft celebrates
Pale Hecate's offerings; and withered Murder,

2.2 A courtyard within Macbeth's castle

Macbeth goes off to murder Duncan. His wife has drugged the King's bodyguards and has placed their daggers ready for Macbeth to use upon the sleeping king.

Activities

B This soliloquy enables us (a) to understand Macbeth's uncertainties about the existence of the dagger; and (b) to form a vivid picture in our minds of 'withered Murder' striding through the blackness of the night. Discuss:

- what we learn about the position of the dagger in the air (33–34); its changing appearance (40–41, 45–46); and the way it behaves (42–43)
- Macbeth's doubts about what he is 'seeing' (35–39, 44–45, 47–49)
- the picture he creates in his mind of the blackness of night and the idea of murder (49–56).

C Look back at the activity on Macbeth's first soliloquy on page 32 in which you discovered how hesitant and disjointed Macbeth's argument was, with its lists of doubts about the afterlife and the reasons for not killing such a good king as Duncan.

Then look at this soliloquy which, by contrast, has a flowing movement, and find the points where the language is all about movement, and is showing us how Macbeth is being led onwards towards the deed (33, 42–43, 54–56, 57).

What might this contrast suggest about Macbeth's different states of mind at these two stages of the play? Why has he changed, in your opinion?

58 prate of my where-about gossip about where I am going

59–60 take the present horror ... and break the horrifying silence which suits what I am going to do

60 threat threaten *('while I talk, rather than act, he's still alive')*

61 Words to ... Words cool down the passion (**heat**) of deeds.

63 knell funeral bell

2 What hath quenched ... The drink which has made them unconscious has given me courage.

3 owl *a bird of the night and of ill omen, compared with the* **bellman** *who rang the bell before an execution*

4 about it performing the murder

5–6 surfeited grooms ... The drunken servingmen make a mockery of their job of guarding the King (**their charge**).

6 possets *late-night alcoholic drinks*

7–8 That death ... *She imagines the figures of Life and Death fighting to determine the fate of the servants.*

8 (***Within***) from just offstage

10–11 the attempt ... Confounds us *If Macbeth has been caught, they will be ruined by attempting the killing rather than actually doing it.*

Alarumed by his sentinel, the wolf,
Whose howl's his watch, thus with his stealthy pace,
With Tarquin's ravishing strides, towards his
    design   55
Moves like a ghost. – Thou sure and firm-set earth,
Hear not my steps, which way they walk, for fear
Thy very stones prate of my where-about,
And take the present horror from the time,
Which now suits with it. Whiles I threat, he lives: 60
Words to the heat of deeds too cold breath gives.

A bell rings.

I go, and it is done: the bell invites me.
Hear it not, Duncan; for it is a knell
That summons thee to heaven or to hell.

                                                  Exit.

Scene 2

The same.

Enter LADY MACBETH.

LADY MACBETH	That which hath made them drunk hath made me
	    bold.
	What hath quenched them hath given me fire. – Hark!
	    – Peace!
	It was the owl that shrieked, the fatal bellman,
	Which gives the stern'st good-night. He is about it.
	The doors are open, and the surfeited grooms 5
	Do mock their charge with snores. I have drugged
	    their possets,
	That death and nature do contend about them,
	Whether they live or die.

MACBETH	(*Within*) Who's there? – what, ho!
LADY MACBETH	Alack! I am afraid they have awaked, And 't is not done: – the attempt, and not the deed, 10 Confounds us. – Hark! – I laid their daggers ready; He could not miss them. – Had he not resembled

2.2 A courtyard within Macbeth's castle

Macbeth returns from killing Duncan, his hands covered in blood, greatly disturbed by his inability to say 'Amen'.

Activities

Actors' interpretations (6)

1. **Macbeth's entrance**: Here is a description of the eighteenth-century actor David Garrick entering (line 14) as Macbeth: 'The door opened and Macbeth appeared, a frightful figure of horror, rushing out sideways with one dagger, and his face in consternation, presented to the door, as if he were pursued, and the other dagger lifted up as presented for action. Thus he stood as if transfixed, seeming insensible to everything but the chamber, unconscious of any presence else, and even to his wife's address of "my husband".'

   Draw a rough sketch which illustrates this description and discuss what kind of impression Garrick was aiming at.

   Some actors do not reveal their bloody hands until just before 'This is a sorry sight' (line 18). What might be the advantages of delaying until this moment?

(Continued on page 48)

13 **I had done't** I would have done it myself

15 **crickets** *Like the owl (line 3, 15) and the raven (1.5.37), another creature of ill omen.*

18 **sorry** miserable

20–27 **There's one ...** *Macbeth might be referring to the two grooms in lines 20–23, but lines 23–27 refer to Malcolm and Donalbain, the King's sons.*

21 **That** so that

22 **addressed them** got ready

23 **lodged together** sleeping in the same room

25 **As** as if

hangman's hands *A hangman's hands were bloody from pulling out the victims' entrails and then cutting the body up.*

Brid Brennan and Roger Allum as Lady Macbeth and Macbeth in 1996

My father as he slept, I had done 't. – My husband!

Enter MACBETH.

MACBETH	I have done the deed. – Didst thou not hear a noise?
LADY MACBETH	I heard the owl scream, and the crickets cry. 15 Did not you speak?
MACBETH	When?
LADY MACBETH	Now.
MACBETH	As I descended?
LADY MACBETH	Ay.
MACBETH	Hark! Who lies i' the second chamber?
LADY MACBETH	Donalbain.
MACBETH	(*Looking at his hands*) This is a sorry sight.
LADY MACBETH	A foolish thought, to say a sorry sight.

MACBETH	There's one did laugh in 's sleep, and one cried,
	    "Murder!" 20
	That they did wake each other: I stood and heard
	    them;
	But they did say their prayers, and addressed them
	Again to sleep.

LADY MACBETH	There are two lodged together.
MACBETH	One cried, "God bless us!" and, "Amen," the other, As they had seen me with these hangman's hands. 25 Listening their fear, I could not say, "Amen," When they did say, "God bless us!"
LADY MACBETH	Consider it not so deeply.

2.2 A courtyard within Macbeth's castle

Macbeth is shaken by having heard a voice telling him that he would never sleep again. In his distraction, he has brought the daggers with him. When he refuses to take them back, Lady Macbeth angrily says she will do it herself.

Activities

2. **Their shattered nerves:** Line 16 is divided into four speeches: 'Did not ... descended?' It is then followed by two other short utterances and a quick question: 'Ay ... chamber?'

In pairs, rehearse lines 14 to 18 (from 'I have done the deed ...' to 'Donalbain'), until you know the speeches well enough not to need the script in your hands. Then practise 'cue-biting' (jumping in with your line before the previous speaker has quite finished theirs). Finally perform the exchange, bringing out the jitteriness in the characters which the verse suggests.

Actors' interpretations (7)

A film version might decide to show the moments that Macbeth describes in lines 20–40 (the grooms waking up and Macbeth hearing a voice cry 'Sleep no more ... !'). In fours, improvise the reported scene for a film version, making decisions about how to represent the 'voice', and including all of its speeches.

Discuss (a) what such a scene could add to a film version; and (b) why you think Shakespeare chose not to portray it in action on stage.

28 **wherefore** why

29 *Macbeth had* **most need of blessing** *because he was about to sin.*

31 **After these ways** in this way

33 **murder sleep** *Sleep (personified) is 'murdered' because: (1) Macbeth killed the sleeping Duncan; and (2) Macbeth will never be able to sleep again.*

34–37 **Sleep ...** Sleep puts right worries, just as someone separates threads of silk (**sleave**) which have become tangled up (**ravelled**). Sleep is the **death of each day's life**; the bath which eases the aches from hard work (**sore labour**); the soothing oil (**balm**) for troubled minds; the main (**second**) course and most important food (**Chief nourisher**) in life's feast.

39–40 *Macbeth is Thane of Glamis and Thane of Cawdor.*

42 **unbend** weaken *(as though straightening a bow: cf 1.7.79)*

43 **so brainsickly** as though you were delirious, or in a fever

44 **filthy witness** evidence of horrible deeds *(the tell-tale blood)*

49–52 **Infirm of purpose!...** *She accuses him of being weak-willed: only children are afraid of nasty pictures.*

53 **gild** paint with ... gold. *There is a pun on 'gilt' (gold covering) and 'guilt'.*

MACBETH	But wherefore could not I pronounce "Amen"? I had most need of blessing, and "Amen" Stuck in my throat.

LADY MACBETH	These deeds must not be thought 30 After these ways: so, it will make us mad.

MACBETH	Methought I heard a voice cry, "Sleep no more! Macbeth does murder sleep," – the innocent sleep; Sleep, that knits up the ravelled sleave of care, The death of each day's life, sore labour's bath, 35 Balm of hurt minds, great nature's second course, Chief nourisher in life's feast; –

LADY MACBETH	What do you mean?

MACBETH	Still it cried, "Sleep no more!" to all the house:
	"Glamis hath murdered sleep, and therefore
	    Cawdor
	Shall sleep no more, Macbeth shall sleep no
	    more!" 40

LADY MACBETH	Who was it that thus cried? Why, worthy thane, You do unbend your noble strength, to think So brainsickly of things. Go, get some water, And wash this filthy witness from your hand. – Why did you bring these daggers from the place? 45 They must lie there; go, carry them, and smear The sleepy grooms with blood.

MACBETH	I'll go no more: I am afraid to think what I have done; Look on 't again I dare not.

LADY MACBETH	Infirm of purpose! Give me the daggers. The sleeping and the dead 50 Are but as pictures; 't is the eye of childhood That fears a painted devil. If he do bleed, I'll gild the faces of the grooms withal, For it must seem their guilt.

Exit.

Knocking within.

2.3 A courtyard within Macbeth's castle

As a knocking is heard on the castle gates, Lady Macbeth returns, but her husband is already regretting what he has done. The castle porter goes to open the door.

Activities

Character review: Macbeth (8)

Discuss and make notes on the changes that have come over Macbeth since the end of 2.1. What is revealed by the following?

- his four brief questions upon entering (2.2.14–17)
- his first reaction to looking at the blood on his hands (18)
- his account of the waking grooms and his inability to say 'amen' (20–30)
- the voice which cried 'Sleep no more . . .!' (32–40)
- his refusal to take the daggers back (47–49)
- his reaction to the knock at the door (54–54)
- the second reaction to looking at the blood (56–60)
- his two final lines (70–71).

Using your notes, and any other ideas you have, write a short piece on 'The initial effects upon Macbeth of killing Duncan.'

---

56 **they pluck out . . .** *He wants to pluck his eyes out, so that he can't see his bloody hands.*

58–60 **this my hand . . .** *My hand is more likely to (**will rather**) turn the countless (**multitudinous**) green seas blood-red (**incarnadine** is a verb).*

61–62 **but I shame . . .** *but I am ashamed to have such a cowardly (**white**) heart*

65–66 **Your constancy . . .** *Your firmness of purpose has deserted you.*

67–68 **lest occasion . . .** *in case an occasion arises to call us and people realise we have been up and awake*

1–2 **porter of hell-gate** *The porter imagines that he is porter of the gates of hell and lists (lines 4–16) some of the people who ask to be let in to hell.*

2 **have old . . .** *He'd have a right old time, always turning the key.*

4–6 **Here's a farmer . . .** *The farmer had hoarded his corn, hoping for a famine, so that he could sell it for a high price, but a good harvest (**the expectation of plenty**) has led to a drop in the price, and he has committed suicide. Because he depends on the seasons, he is a **time-server** (and will also 'serve time' in hell).*

MACBETH	Whence is that knocking? –

MACBETH   Whence is that knocking? –
How is 't with me, when every noise appals me?   55
What hands are here? Ha! they pluck out mine eyes.
Will all great Neptune's ocean wash this blood
Clean from my hand? No, this my hand will rather
The multitudinous seas incarnadine,
Making the green one red.   60

Re-enter LADY MACBETH.

LADY
MACBETH My hands are of your colour; but I shame
To wear a heart so white. (*Knock*) I hear a knocking
At the south entry: retire we to our chamber.
A little water clears us of this deed:
How easy is it then! Your constancy   65
Hath left you unattended. – (*Knock*) Hark! more
    knocking.
Get on your night-gown, lest occasion call us,
And show us to be watchers. – Be not lost
So poorly in your thoughts.

MACBETH   To know my deed, 't were best not know myself.   70

Knock.

Wake Duncan with thy knocking: I would thou
    couldst!

                                            Exeunt.

Scene 3

The same.

Enter a PORTER.

Knocking within.

PORTER   Here's a knocking indeed! If a man were porter of
hell-gate, he should have old turning the key.
(*Knocking*) Knock, knock, knock. Who's there, i'
the name of Beelzebub? – Here's a farmer that
hanged himself on the expectation of plenty;   5
come in time-server; have napkins enough about

2.3 A courtyard within Macbeth's castle

The porter imagines himself to be the porter of hell-gate, welcoming various types of sinner. He admits Macduff and Lenox and jokes with them about the effects of alcohol.

Activities

Actors' interpretations (8)

What do you imagine the porter to look like? Study this photograph and discuss what you can tell from his appearance about the way in which he might have been performed on stage. Then discuss what the porter would look like in a production of your own.

Adrian Schiller as the porter in 1996

9–13 **an equivocator** ... *someone who does not actually lie, but does not tell the whole truth*

9–12 **swear in both the scales** ... He could balance up the scales of Justice, by arguing on both sides, and prevent someone from being convicted; but he could not argue his way in (**equivocate**) to heaven.

14–15 *Tailors were known for making a profit by using less cloth than the customer had paid for; but when the new-style tight-fitting French breeches (**French hose**) came in, he was caught.*

20–21 **the primrose way** ... *The path to hell (**the everlasting bonfire**) is imagined as being very attractive and seductive, covered in spring flowers.*

25 **carousing** ... partying until about three in the morning (**the second cock**)

26 **provoker** instigator, encourager

28 **nose-painting** getting a red nose *(through drink)*

32–37 **an equivocator with lechery** ... it makes a man feel virile, but ruins (**mars**) him; makes him lustful (**sets him on ... persuades him ... makes him stand to ...**), but prevents him getting an erection (**takes him off ... disheartens him ... not stand to**); it satisfies his lust only in a dream (**equivocates him in a sleep**) and, having deceived him, leaves him

you; here you'll sweat for 't. (*Knocking*) Knock,
knock. Who's there, i' the other devil's name? –
'Faith, here's an equivocator that could swear in
both the scales against either scale; who   10
committed treason enough for God's sake, yet
could not equivocate to heaven: O! come in,
equivocator. (*Knocking*) Knock, knock, knock.
Who's there? – 'Faith, here's an English tailor
come hither for stealing out of a French hose: 15
come in, tailor; here you may roast your goose.
(*Knocking*) Knock, knock. Never at quiet! What
are you? – But this place is too cold for hell. I'll
devil-porter it no further: I had thought to have
let in some of all professions that go the primrose   20
way to the everlasting bonfire. (*Knocking*) Anon,
anon: I pray you, remember the porter.

Opens the gate.

Enter MACDUFF and LENOX.

MACDUFF	Was it so late, friend, ere you went to bed,
	That you do lie so late?

PORTER	'Faith, Sir, we were carousing till the second cock; 25
	and drink, Sir, is a great provoker of three things.

MACDUFF	What three things does drink especially provoke?

PORTER	Marry, Sir, nose-painting, sleep and urine.
	Lechery, Sir, it provokes and unprovokes: it
	provokes the desire, but it takes away the 30
	performance. Therefore, much drink may be said
	to be an equivocator with lechery: it makes him
	and it mars him; it sets him on, and it takes him
	off; it persuades him, and disheartens him; makes
	him stand to, and not stand to: in conclusion, 35
	equivocates him in a sleep, and, giving him the
	lie, leaves him.

MACDUFF	I believe drink gave thee the lie last night.

PORTER	That it did, Sir, i' the very throat o' me: but I
	requited him for his lie; and, I think, being too 40

2.3 A courtyard within Macbeth's castle

Macbeth enters and shows Macduff where Duncan is lodging. Lenox describes the strange unnatural events of the previous night.

Activities

Shakespeare's language: short speeches and tension

Lines 43–54 are made up of a series of short speeches. In groups of three, act out the rapid exchange, bringing out the tension and sense of audience anticipation. Think carefully about how Macbeth might say 'He does: – he did appoint so.'

Actors' interpretations (9): difficult lines

Coming after Lenox's frightening and dramatic description, Macbeth's line (62) can get a laugh if it is not handled carefully. According to one reviewer, Laurence Olivier's Macbeth listened to Lenox's account from the other side of the stage – as far away from Duncan's death-chamber as he could get – silently nodding throughout as if in confirmation of the horror. When Lenox stopped talking, there was a brief but awful pause; Olivier's head stopped shaking, he looked towards Duncan's chamber and then said '"T was a rough night' as if it were a curse.

Try performing the moment in this way and discuss the effect. Consider other ways in which the line might be delivered and compare them with Olivier's performance.

41 **took up my legs** kicked my legs from under me *(like a wrestler)*

42 **made a shift to** managed to

cast (1) throw *(as in wrestling)*; (2) throw up

47 **timely** early

48 **slipped** missed

49 **joyful trouble** *because the King's visit has been a trouble, but one that Macbeth has enjoyed*

51 **The labour ...** Work that we enjoy is a cure for (**physics**) any hardship (**pain**) it causes.

53 **my limited service** my appointed duty

54 **hence** from here ('Is the King leaving today?')

55 **unruly** wild and stormy; *because the murder of a king is against nature, nature is causing 'unnatural' things to happen*

57 **Lamentings** cries of misery

59–60 **dire combustion ...** terrible confusion in the land, chaotic happenings (**confused events**), newborn (**New hatched**) to the sad time.

60–61 **The obscure bird ...** The owl ('the bird of darkness') hooted (**Clamoured**) throughout the night.

strong for him, though he took up my legs
sometime, yet I made a shift to cast him.

MACDUFF Is thy master stirring?

Enter MACBETH.

Our knocking has awaked him; here he comes.

LENOX (*To MACBETH*) Good morrow, noble Sir!

MACBETH   Good morrow, both! 45

MACDUFF Is the king stirring, worthy thane?

MACBETH   Not yet.

MACDUFF He did command me to call timely on him:
I have almost slipped the hour.

MACBETH   I'll bring you to him.

MACDUFF I know this is a joyful trouble to you;
But yet 't is one.   50

MACBETH The labour we delight in physics pain.
This is the door.

MACDUFF   I'll make so bold to call.
For 't is my limited service.

                                        Exit.

LENOX Goes the king hence today?

MACBETH   He does: – he did appoint so.

LENOX The night has been unruly: where we lay,   55
Our chimneys were blown down; and, as they say,
Lamentings heard i' the air; strange screams of
   death,
And prophesying with accents terrible
Of dire combustion, and confused events,
New hatched to the woeful time. The obscure bird   60
Clamoured the livelong night: some say the earth

2.3 A courtyard within Macbeth's castle

Macduff enters, crying out in horror at his discovery of Duncan's murder. As Lenox and Macbeth go to see the sight for themselves, Lady Macbeth enters.

Activities

Character review: Lady Macbeth (3)

Lady Macbeth clearly has to enter the scene determined to deceive everybody and help her husband shift the blame for the murder on to Duncan's grooms. Look at the following moments and write notes to show what thoughts might be going through her head:

- her entrance (82)
- her reaction to the news of Duncan's murder (88–89)
- her feelings on seeing her husband enter (92)
- her reaction to Macbeth's first words (92–97)
- her feelings on seeing Duncan's sons enter (98)
- her changing thoughts as she remains silent for a while, listening to Macbeth's admission that he killed the grooms (108–109)
- her reaction to Macbeth's account of finding the dead King (110–120).

In particular, discuss the important question: is Lady Macbeth's faint (120) real or put on? If real, what has caused it? If it is faked, why does she do it?

63–64 **My young remembrance . . .** I cannot recall a night like it (in my short life).

67 **Confusion** destruction

68–69 **Most sacrilegious murder . . .** *Duncan would be thought of as God's representative on earth (**anointed** with holy oil when crowned), and so to kill him would be sacrilege.*

73 **Gorgon** *In Greek mythology anyone who looked at a Gorgon was turned to stone; looking on Duncan's body would have a comparable effect.*

77 **downy** comfortable *(on pillows stuffed with down)*

counterfeit imitation

79–80 **The great doom's image . . .** a sight as terrifying as the Last Judgement, when spirits of the dead (**sprites**) rise from their graves

81 **countenance** (1) be in keeping with; (2) behold, face

83 **calls to parley** *like a trumpet in wartime, calling the armies together for talks*

Was feverous, and did shake.

MACBETH   'T was a rough night.

LENOX   My young remembrance cannot parallel
             A fellow to it.

Re-enter MACDUFF.

MACDUFF   O horror! horror! horror! Tongue, nor heart,   65
             Cannot conceive, nor name thee!

MACBETH   What's the matter?
AND LENOX

MACDUFF   Confusion now hath made his masterpiece!
             Most sacrilegious murder hath broke ope
             The Lord's anointed temple, and stole thence
             The life o' the building!

MACBETH   What is 't you say? the life?   70

LENOX   Mean you his majesty?

MACDUFF   Approach the chamber, and destroy your sight
             With a new Gorgon. – Do not bid me speak:
             See, and then speak yourselves. –

                                Exeunt MACBETH and LENOX.

                                       Awake! awake! –
             Ring the alarum-bell. – Murder and treason!   75
             Banquo and Donalbain! Malcolm! awake!
             Shake off this downy sleep, death's counterfeit,
             And look on death itself! – up, up, and see
             The great doom's image! – Malcolm! Banquo!
             As from your graves rise up, and walk like sprites 80
             To countenance this horror! Ring the bell.

Bell rings.

Enter LADY MACBETH.

LADY   What's the business,
MACBETH   That such a hideous trumpet calls to parley
             The sleepers of the house? speak, speak!

A courtyard within Macbeth's castle

Macbeth returns and expresses his shock. Duncan's sons, Malcolm and Donalbain, are told of their father's murder at the hands, it seems, of his bodyguards.

Activities

Actors' interpretations (10): difficult lines

Just like ''T was a rough night', there are other moments in this scene when an exchange can easily sound comic. Perform the following in different ways to discover what effects can be achieved:

- Lady Macbeth's reaction to the news that Duncan has been murdered: 'What! in our house?' (89)
- Macbeth's reply to Donalbain's question 'What is amiss?': 'You are, and do not know 't'(98)
- Malcolm's response to the news that his father has been murdered: 'O! by whom?'(101).

Actors' interpretations (11): reacting to the question

There is an extremely dramatic moment when Malcolm asks 'O! by whom?' (101)

A Freeze-frame the moment, showing very clearly how every character should react: how does each one feel? where do they look? who already suspects Macbeth, and who believes his story that the grooms were responsible?

(Continued on page 60)

86–87 The repetition ... reporting it to a woman would kill her

90 I pr'ythee I beg you, 'I pray thee'

92–97 Had I but died ... *Although Macbeth is trying to cover up, he is revealing something which we know to be true: it would have been better had he died before the murder.*

92 before this chance before this happened

94 nothing serious in mortality nothing important in human life

95 toys trivial things

renown fame

96–97 The wine of life ... *Macbeth thinks of life as a wine cellar* (**vault**), *in which the best wine has been taken from the cask* (**drawn**) *and all that is left to boast about* (**brag of**) *is the dregs* (**lees**).

98 What is amiss? What's wrong?

99–100 The spring ... *He compares Duncan to the source of a river which has been blocked off.*

102 *Notice Lenox's* **as it seemed**.

MACDUFF   O gentle lady,
            'T is not for you to hear what I can speak: 85
            The repetition, in a woman's ear,
            Would murder as it fell.

Enter BANQUO.

                                    O Banquo! Banquo!
            Our royal master's murdered!

LADY   Woe, alas!
    MACBETH   What! in our house?

BANQUO   Too cruel anywhere.
            Dear Duff, I pr'ythee, contradict thyself,   90
            And say it is not so.

Re-enter MACBETH and LENOX.

MACBETH   Had I but died an hour before this chance,
            I had lived a blessed time; for, from this instant,
            There's nothing serious in mortality;
            All is but toys: renown, and grace, is dead;   95
            The wine of life is drawn, and the mere lees
            Is left this vault to brag of.

Enter MALCOLM and DONALBAIN.

DONALBAIN   What is amiss?

MACBETH   You are, and do not know 't:
            The spring, the head, the fountain of your blood
            Is stopped; the very source of it is stopped.   100

MACDUFF   Your royal father's murdered.

MALCOLM   O! by whom?

LENOX   Those of his chamber, as it seemed, had done 't:
            Their hands and faces were all badged with blood;
            So were their daggers, which, unwiped, we found
            Upon their pillows: 105
            They stared, and were distracted; no man's life
            Was to be trusted with them.

2.3 A courtyard within Macbeth's castle

Macbeth explains why he killed the bodyguards. As he describes his vision of the murdered Duncan, his wife faints and is carried out. Duncan's sons privately show their fears for their own safety.

Activities

B Draw a diagram, showing how the moment might be 'blocked' on stage (what positions the actors have taken up), with notes to indicate how each character is behaving.

C Act out lines 82–101: (a) to show that neither Lady Macbeth nor Macbeth is very successful in deceiving the others (e.g. both of them 'overacting'); then (b) to show them as very skilful deceivers. Discuss which of the two interpretations you prefer, in terms of what you know of the characters and the story so far.

108–109 *The audience learns that Macbeth has killed Duncan's servants at the same time as Macduff and the others do.*

112–113 **The expedition ...** My passionate love for the King caused me to act hastily, before reason could make me stop and think.

115–116 **a breach ...** a gaping hole in the natural world, through which death (**ruin**) could make its destructive (**wasteful**) entrance

122 **That most may claim ...** So that most people can claim that this is our doing?

124–125 **... auger-hole ...** *Donalbain fears that danger may be treacherously hidden in the smallest place, such as the tiny hole made by a carpenter's tool (**auger**).*

126–127 **Nor our strong sorrow ...** Our powerful sorrow is stronger than it appears; it has not yet begun to take action.

128 **our naked frailties** our bodies which are weak when undressed

132–134 **In the great hand ...** I put myself in God's protection, and relying on God (**thence**), I will fight against the hidden purposes (**undivulged pretence**) of malicious traitors.

MACBETH	O! yet I do repent me of my fury That I did kill them.
MACDUFF	Wherefore did you so?
MACBETH	Who can be wise, amazed, temperate and furious, 110 Loyal and neutral, in a moment? No man: The expedition of my violent love Outran the pauser reason. – Here lay Duncan, His silver skin laced with his golden blood; And his gashed stabs looked like a breach in nature 115 For ruin's wasteful entrance: there, the murderers, Steeped in the colours of their trade, their daggers Unmannerly breeched with gore. Who could refrain, That had a heart to love, and in that heart Courage, to make's love known?
LADY MACBETH	(*Fainting*) Help me hence, ho! 120
MACDUFF	Look to the lady.
MALCOLM	(*Aside to* DONALBAIN) Why do we hold our tongues, That most may claim this argument for ours?
DONALBAIN	(*Aside to* MALCOLM) What should be spoken Here where our fate, hid in an auger-hole, May rush and seize us? Let's away: our tears 125 Are not yet brewed.
MALCOLM	(*Aside to* DONALBAIN) Nor our strong sorrow Upon the foot of motion.
BANQUO	Look to the lady: –

LADY MACBETH is carried out.

	And when we have our naked frailties hid, That suffer in exposure, let us meet, And question this most bloody piece of work, 130 To know it further. Fears and scruples shake us: In the great hand of God I stand; and thence Against the undivulged pretence I fight Of treasonous malice.

2.4 Outside Macbeth's castle

Malcolm plans to flee to England, Donalbain to Ireland. An Old Man and Rosse discuss the murder.

Activities

Character review: Malcolm (1)

Look back at lines 98 onwards and discuss (a) whether you think Malcolm now knows who murdered his father; (b) which of the thanes he feels he can trust, if any; (c) exactly why he thinks that running away is his best policy; (d) what practical steps he can now take to claim the throne which is rightfully his.

Actors' interpretations (12): the Old Man

Who is this old man? He is not identified by name and does not appear anywhere else in the play. Consider the following questions as you read the scene:

1. Does he represent ordinary people's opinions of what is going on among the thanes and the royal family?
2. Is he a kind of commentator (like the 'chorus' figure that Shakespeare includes in plays such as *Henry V* and *Romeo and Juliet*)?
3. Is there any argument for having another named character play this part (such as one of the other thanes)?

135 **put on manly readiness** (1) get properly dressed; (2) adopt a warlike frame of mind

137 **consort** keep company

138 **office** job

142–143 **There's daggers ...** People who appear friendly are dangerous; and the more closely we are related to them (**the near in blood**), the more dangerous they are.

143–145 **This murderous shaft ...** This murderous arrow has not yet hit its target (**lighted**); it's safest to keep out of its way (**avoid the aim**).

146 **... dainty of leave-taking** Let's not be fussy about saying goodbye properly.

147–148 **There's warrant ...** When there are merciless people around, stealing away is a justifiable ('*warranted*') kind of stealing.

1 **Threescore and ten** 70 years

3–4 **this sore night ...** This dreadful night has made everything I have experienced before (**former knowings**) seem trivial (**Hath trifled**).

5–6 **Thou seest, the heavens ...** You see the heavens, as though disturbed by men's deeds, are now threatening the earth (**act** and **stage** are clearly theatrical terms; so is **heavens** – the painted canopy above the stage).

MACDUFF	And so do I.
ALL	So all.
MACBETH	Let's briefly put on manly readiness, 135
	And meet i' the hall together.
ALL	Well contented.

Exeunt all but MALCOLM and DONALBAIN.

MALCOLM	What will you do? Let's not consort with them:
	To show an unfelt sorrow is an office
	Which the false man does easy. I'll to England.
DONALBAIN	To Ireland, I: our separated fortune 140
	Shall keep us both the safer; where we are
	There's daggers in men's smiles; the near in blood,
	The nearer bloody.
MALCOLM	This murderous shaft that's shot
	Hath not yet lighted, and our safest way
	Is to avoid the aim: therefore, to horse, 145
	And let us not be dainty of leave-taking,
	But shift away. There's warrant in that theft
	Which steals itself, when there's no mercy left.

Exeunt.

Scene 4

Outside the castle.

Enter ROSSE and an OLD MAN.

OLD MAN	Threescore and ten I can remember well;
	Within the volume of which time I have seen
	Hours dreadful and things strange, but this sore
	night
	Hath trifled former knowings.
ROSSE	Ha, good father,
	Thou seest, the heavens, as troubled with man's
	act, 5
	Threatens his bloody stage: by the clock 't is day,

2.4 Outside Macbeth's castle

Rosse and the Old Man talk about the disturbing unnatural events that have accompanied the murder. Macduff joins them and reports that Duncan's sons have been accused of bribing the bodyguards.

Activities

Themes: nature and the unnatural

Lenox's description of the previous night's strange happenings in 2.3.55–62 and those by Rosse and the Old Man here (1–20) are similar to one in Shakespeare's *Julius Caesar* where, as in *Macbeth*, disturbances in the natural world seem to reflect – or even be reacting to – the unnatural killing of a king or leader ('unnatural' means 'against the laws of nature'). The Roman Casca reports (1.3) having seen a slave with his hand on fire but not burned, a lion outside the Capitol (the main government building in Rome), terrified women claiming they had seen men of fire walking through the streets, and an owl hooting at noon; while Caesar's wife Calphurnia has heard (2.2) of a lioness giving birth in the streets, graves opening to give up their dead, warriors fighting in the clouds and drizzling blood upon the Capitol, horses neighing, dying men groaning and ghosts shrieking through the streets.

(Continued on page 66)

7 **travelling lamp** the sun, as it journeys across the sky

8 **Is 't night's predominance ...** Is it the superior power of night *(the darkness of evil)*? Or is the day hiding its face in shame?

10–18 **'T is unnatural ...** *Again (see 2.3.55–64), the suggestion is made that nature is reflecting the 'unnatural' act of murdering a king with freakish weather and strange animal behaviour.*

12 **towering ...** climbing through the air to its highest point (**pride of place**)

13 **mousing owl ...** *The owl would normally be flying nearer the ground in search of prey.*

15 **minions of their race** 'darlings' of their breed

17 **Contending 'gainst obedience** rebelling against their training

24 **What good could they pretend?** What could they possibly hope to gain by it?

24 **suborned** bribed, persuaded to commit the crime

27 **'Gainst nature still** yet another example of unnatural behaviour

28–29 **Thriftless ...** Profitless ambition, which will voraciously eat up (**ravin up**) the body that gives you life! *(By killing the King – allegedly – the King's sons have destroyed the system by which they could themselves inherit the throne.)*

29 **'t is most like** it is most likely that

And yet dark night strangles the travelling lamp.
Is 't night's predominance, or the day's shame,
That darkness does the face of earth entomb,
When living light should kiss it?

OLD MAN   'T is unnatural,   10
Even like the deed that's done. On Tuesday last,
A falcon, towering in her pride of place,
Was by a mousing owl hawked at, and killed.

ROSSE   And Duncan's horses (a thing most strange and
                certain)
Beauteous and swift, the minions of their race,   15
Turned wild in nature, broke their stalls, flung out,
Contending 'gainst obedience, as they would make
War with mankind.

OLD MAN   'T is said, they ate each other.

ROSSE   They did so, to th' amazement of mine eyes,
That looked upon 't –

Enter MACDUFF.

                              Here comes the good Macduff. – 20
How goes the world, Sir, now?

MACDUFF   Why, see you not?

ROSSE   Is 't known, who did this more than bloody deed?

MACDUFF   Those that Macbeth hath slain.

ROSSE   Alas, the day!
What good could they pretend?

MACDUFF   They were suborned.
Malcolm and Donalbain, the king's two sons,   25
Are stol'n away and fled; which puts upon them
Suspicion of the deed.

ROSSE   'Gainst nature still:
Thriftless Ambition, that wilt ravin up
Thine own life's means! – Then 't is most like
The sovereignty will fall upon Macbeth.   30

2.4 Outside Macbeth's castle

Macduff reports that Macbeth has already gone to Scone to be crowned as King. Rosse plans to attend the coronation btut Macduff is returning home to Fife.

<table>
<tr><td>

Activities

(A) Discuss what all these strange events have in common. The clue is in the Old Man's comment: ''T is unnatural, Even like the deed that's done' (10–11).

(B) Either (a) annotate Lenox's, Rosse's and the Old Man's lines with suggested sound effects and music for a radio version (and record the sequences if you can); or (b) create a collage which reflects the scenes they describe.

(C) Discuss other features of the language and the plot in Acts 1 and 2 which seem to contribute to this theme by their references to nature and natural growth (e.g. 1.3.58–59; 1.4.28–29) and the ways in which the natural order of events is being turned upside down (e.g. 1.3.141–142; 1.5.39–53).

Actors' interpretations (13): Rosse

In the film version directed by Roman Polanski, Rosse is played as a treacherous thane who supports Macbeth, in the full knowledge that he has murdered for the crown. In groups of three perform the scene, and discuss how Rosse's lines might be interpreted if he is played as pro-Macbeth. What might the actor do to make this interpretation clear to the audience?

</td></tr>
</table>

31 **named** chosen as king

31–33 *Scone* was where Scottish kings were crowned (**invested**); **Colme-kill** *(Iona) was where they were buried.*

36 *Macduff was Thane of* **Fife**.

36 **I will thither** I will go there *(to Scone)*

38 **Lest our old robes ...** *Just as old clothes are more comfortable* (**sit easier**) *than new ones, so the old regime of Duncan might prove better to live under than Macbeth's.*

40 **benison** blessing

MACDUFF   He is already named, and gone to Scone
          To be invested.

ROSSE   Where is Duncan's body?

MACDUFF   Carried to Colme-kill,
          The sacred storehouse of his predecessors,
          And guardian of their bones.

ROSSE   Will you to Scone?   35

MACDUFF   No, cousin; I'll to Fife.

ROSSE   Well, I will thither.

MACDUFF   Well, may you see things well done there: – adieu! –
          Lest our old robes sit easier than our new!

ROSSE   Farewell, father.

OLD MAN   God's benison go with you; and with those   40
          That would make good of bad, and friends of foes!

                                                Exeunt.

Exam practice

Plot review (2)

(A) Draw up a time line to represent the main events so far, starting with the battle and ending with Macbeth's coronation. First discuss which main facts ought to be represented, and work out how much time has elapsed since just before the play began (when the battle was being fought) until Rosse's departure for Scone.

(B) Write Banquo's thoughts as he ponders all the events since the battle, including his secret opinions about what happened the night of Duncan's murder, and his fears; he might also express concerns about Malcolm and about Scotland's future.

(C) Unlike Shakespeare's other major tragedies, *Macbeth* does not have a sub-plot: everything centres upon the story of Macbeth's career. Write a brief account of the facts established so far which are clearly going to affect Macbeth in the rest of the play. Include:
- the Witches' prophecies and their apparent influence
- the situation in which Banquo finds himself
- the personalities of both Macbeth and Lady Macbeth, as they are revealed both before and after the murder
- the fact that Malcolm has escaped.

Character review: the relationship between Macbeth (9) and Lady Macbeth (4)

Re-read the statements below, which are about Act 2, and produce detailed responses to each statement:
- Macbeth always confides in his wife and shares his innermost thoughts with her.
- They are both capable of taking practical steps in getting what they want.
- They always support each other.
- Lady Macbeth always tries to build her husband's confidence.
- When things get difficult, Macbeth is stronger-willed than his wife.
- In 2.3 they are both good at covering up their guilt.
- From the events of Act 2, it looks as though Macbeth and his wife will be a successful partnership as the new rulers of Scotland.

You should:
- decide whether you agree or disagree with each statement
- choose one or more quotations from the play to support your opinion
- explain in detail why you agree or disagree.

Character review: Macduff (1) and Rosse (1)

Look again at 2.4.20–41. Read carefully what is being said by each character and think about what they are really thinking or feeling. Then produce the sub-text of the scene, by writing down what the character is thinking or feeling next to the actual text. For example, you might begin:

ROSSE: *Here's Macduff. I will test out whether he is a supporter of Macbeth or not . . .*

Actors' interpretations (14): after the murder

Imagine you are directing a performance of *Macbeth*. Annotate 2.3.54–148 and then use your notes to write detailed instructions to help the actors perform the scene most effectively.
You could give the actors advice on:
- how the characters are feeling, and why
- how they could say particular lines, and why
- movements and actions they could make at certain points, and why
- the reactions you want the audience to have, and why.

Actors' interpretations (15): the dagger

Stage and film productions of *Macbeth* have made a variety of different decisions about how to present Macbeth's imagined dagger. The famous eighteenth-century actor David Garrick is reported to have made audiences imagine that the dagger was actually there, simply by the way in which he stared at it, and traced its shape in the air.

1. Discuss the advantages and disadvantages of (a) a film version in which the audience is required to imagine the dagger, as the actor does; and (b) a version where the supernatural dagger is actually shown floating in front of Macbeth's eyes.
2. What difference does it make if we actually see the dagger?

Shakespeare's language: 'blood'

'Blood' is a key word in the play. To visualise Macbeth's nightmarish vision of never being able to wash the blood off his hand, find images in magazines to create a collage (or paint your own picture) which will represent his fear that 'this my hand will rather The multitudinous seas incarnadine, Making the green one red.' (2.3.58–60)

3.1 A room in the palace

Banquo expresses his fears that Macbeth murdered Duncan and begins to wonder whether the Witches' prophecies to him will also come true. Macbeth asks him where he intends to ride this afternoon.

Activities

Actors' interpretations (16): questioning Banquo

In attempting not to put Banquo on his guard, Macbeth engages in innocent conversation. However, he still manages to insert three crucial and highly significant questions:
- Ride you this afternoon? (19)
- Is 't far you ride? (23)
- Goes Fleance with you? (35).

A Re-read the dialogue (11–39) and discuss what you think lies behind the three questions. Rehearse the conversation and find ways of making the questions sound as innocent as possible.

B To explore how cleverly Macbeth extracts the required information from Banquo, improvise the scene in pairs, inserting the three questions, in your own words, as subtly as you can.

C Annotate the conversation between Macbeth and Banquo to show (a) Macbeth's thoughts; and (b) what the actor might do in order to disguise his intentions. (In some productions, for example, Macbeth has been particularly affectionate towards Fleance, tousling his hair and so on.)

1 **it** the crown

3 **Thou playedst . . .** you played a very dirty game; acted in a most evil way

4 **It should not stand . . .** the crown would not remain in your family; not be passed on to your descendants

6 **them** the Witches

7 **their speeches shine** their prophecies are gloriously fulfilled

8–10 **Why, by the verities . . .?** Why, in line with the things that have come true for you, might the Witches not be my prophets of truth (**oracles**) as well, and give me hope?

Sennet a fanfare of trumpets

13 **all-thing unbecoming** wholly inappropriate

14 **solemn** ceremonial

15–18 **Let your highness . . .** Command me anything; I am tied to you in duty with a knot which cannot be broken (**indissoluble tie**).

20 **else** otherwise

21 **Which still hath been . . .** which has always been serious and profitable

25–27 **go not my horse . . .** If my horse doesn't go faster than that, I might have to take up an hour or two of the night.

Act 3

Scene 1

Forres. A room in the palace.

Enter BANQUO.

BANQUO   Thou hast it now, King, Cawdor, Glamis, all,
As the weird women promised; and, I fear,
Thou playedst most foully for 't; yet it was said,
It should not stand in thy posterity;
But that myself should be the root and father   5
Of many kings. If there come truth from them
(As upon thee, Macbeth, their speeches shine),
Why, by the verities on thee made good,
May they not be my oracles as well,
And set me up in hope? But, hush; no more.   10

*Sennet sounded. Enter MACBETH as King; LADY MACBETH as Queen;
LENOX, ROSSE, lords and attendants.*

MACBETH   Here's our chief guest.

LADY   If he had been forgotten,
MACBETH It had been as a gap in our great feast,
And all-thing unbecoming.

MACBETH   (*To* BANQUO) Tonight we hold a solemn supper, Sir,
And I'll request your presence.

BANQUO   Let your highness   15
Command upon me, to the which my duties
Are with a most indissoluble tie
For ever knit.

MACBETH   Ride you this afternoon?

BANQUO   Ay, my good lord.

MACBETH   We should have else desired your good advice   20
(Which still hath been both grave and prosperous)
In this day's council; but we'll take tomorrow.
Is 't far you ride?

BANQUO   As far, my lord, as will fill up the time
'Twixt this and supper: go not my horse the better,   25

3.1 A room in the palace

Checking that Fleance will be riding with Banquo, Macbeth sends everyone away and considers his fears about Banquo.

Activities

Shakespeare's language: the royal plural (2)

Re-read lines 11–47 and then pick out all the occasions in which Macbeth and his wife – now King and Queen – use the royal plural.

1. What does this show about their view of themselves as Act 3 begins?
2. In a few cases, Macbeth uses the singular: discuss why that should be.

Character review: Banquo (3)

Christopher Ravenscroft, who played Banquo in 1994, said: 'Banquo genuinely doesn't feel that he's in danger himself. It's extraordinary that he comes back to attend Macbeth's banquet – he should go straight away like Macduff does, but I think it's an arrogance or a naivety which makes him feel he is immune from Macbeth's ambition.'

Remind yourself of the prophecies made to Banquo by looking back at 1.3.65–67. Then re-read the statement of Banquo's qualities, as Macbeth describes them in 3.1.48–56, and discuss exactly why Macbeth might be worried about Banquo on account of (a) his character; and (b) the Witches' prophecies.

27 **Fail not** don't miss

29 *Malcolm and Donalbain;* **bestowed** settled

31 **parricide** *the murder of one's father*

32 **strange invention** absurd lies

33–34 **When, therewithal ...** when, in addition, there will be state business (**cause**) which we need to attend to together

34 **Hie you** hurry

36 **our time** it is time for us to go

40 **be master of his time** pass the time as he wishes

41–43 **to make society ...** I will remain alone for now, so that we will enjoy being with each other even more when we meet again at supper.

43 **while then** until that time

44 **Sirrah** You, there! *(A word frequently used to call servants.)*

44–45 **Attend ...?** Are those men waiting to see me?

46 **without** outside

47 **To be thus** to be king

48–53 **Our fears ...** My fear of Banquo is like a thorn in my flesh; and in his natural nobility (**his royalty of nature**) there is much that I am frightened of; he is daring; and, in addition to that fearless temperament (**dauntless temper of his mind**), he possesses a wisdom which guides his bravery (**valour**) to act safely.

> I must become a borrower of the night
> For a dark hour or twain.

| MACBETH | Fail not our feast. |

| BANQUO | My lord, I will not. |

| MACBETH | We hear our bloody cousins are bestowed |

In England and in Ireland; not confessing   30
Their cruel parricide, filling their hearers
With strange invention. But of that tomorrow,
When, therewithal, we shall have cause of state
Craving us jointly. Hie you to horse; adieu,
Till you return at night. Goes Fleance with you?   35

| BANQUO | Ay, my good lord: our time does call upon 's. |

| MACBETH | I wish your horses swift, and sure of foot; |

And so I do commend you to their backs.
Farewell. –

Exit BANQUO.

(*To the lords*) Let every man be master of his time   40
Till seven at night; to make society
The sweeter welcome, we will keep ourself
Till supper-time alone: while then, God be with you.

Exeunt LADY MACBETH, lords, etc.

(*To an* ATTENDANT) Sirrah, a word with you. Attend
   those men
Our pleasure?   45

| ATTENDANT | They are, my lord, without the palace gate. |

| MACBETH | Bring them before us. (*Exit* ATTENDANT) – To be thus is |

   nothing,
But to be safely thus. – Our fears in Banquo
Stick deep, and in his royalty of nature
Reigns that which would be feared; 't is much he
   dares;   50
And, to that dauntless temper of his mind,
He hath a wisdom that doth guide his valour
To act in safety. There is none but he

3.1 A room in the palace

Tormented by the Witches' prophecy that Banquo's descendants would be kings, Macbeth determines to take action. He reminds two murderers of an earlier conversation in which he had proved that it was Banquo who had persecuted them.

Activities

Character review: Macbeth (10)

This speech (47–71) is Macbeth's third soliloquy and, after expressing his feelings about Banquo, he thinks about the Witches' prophecies.

Work in pairs to gain an idea of his fears and worries, using the following as a structure:

It's one thing to be King, but:
- 47–48   . . .

Banquo worries me greatly:
- 48–50   . . .
- 50–53   . . .
- 53–56   . . .

The Witches treated him differently:
- 56–59   . . .
- 60–63   . . .

Have I done all this for nothing?
- 63–67   . . .
- 67–69   . . .

I will defy fate:
- 70–71   . . .

55–56 **My genius** . . . *Banquo makes Macbeth feel inferior.*

60–61 *The crown is* **fruitless** *and the* **sceptre** *(ceremonial staff)* **barren**, *because Macbeth's descendants would not inherit them.*

62 **Thence to be wrenched** . . . to be torn from it by someone who is not one of my descendants

64 **For Banquo's issue** . . . I have polluted (**filed**) my mind for Banquo's descendants.

67–68 **mine eternal jewel** . . . and have given my immortal soul to the devil (**common enemy of man**)

70–71 **Rather than so** . . . Rather than let that happen, I will challenge fate to enter the tournament (**list**) and fight to the death (**to the utterance**) as a champion against me!

76–78 **it was he** . . . It was Banquo who, in earlier days, stopped you enjoying the life you deserved (**held you so under fortune**), and not me, as you thought: I was innocent.

79–83 **passed in probation** . . . I went over the proof of how you were deceived (**borne in hand**), and thwarted (**crossed**); what methods (**instruments**) he used; who was involved (**wrought with them**); and everything else which even a half-wit or mind of a madman (**notion crazed**) could see was Banquo's doing.

Whose being I do fear; and under him
My genius is rebuked, as, it is said,   55
Mark Antony's was by Caesar. He chid the sisters
When first they put the name of king upon me,
And bade them speak to him; then, prophet-like,
They hailed him father to a line of kings.
Upon my head they placed a fruitless crown,   60
And put a barren sceptre in my gripe,
Thence to be wrenched with an unlineal hand,
No son of mine succeeding. If 't be so,
For Banquo's issue have I filed my mind;
For them the gracious Duncan have I murdered;   65
Put rancours in the vessel of my peace
Only for them; and mine eternal jewel
Given to the common enemy of man,
To make them kings, the seed of Banquo kings!
Rather than so, come, fate, into the list,   70
And champion me to the utterance! – Who's there? –

Re-enter ATTENDANT, with two MURDERERS.

(*To the ATTENDANT*) Now, go to the door, and stay there
   till we call.

Exit ATTENDANT.

(*To the MURDERERS*) Was it not yesterday we spoke
   together?

1 MURDERER It was, so please your highness.

MACBETH   Well then, now
Have you considered of my speeches? Know   75
That it was he, in the times past, which held you
So under fortune, which, you thought, had been
Our innocent self. This I made good to you
In our last conference; passed in probation with you
How you were borne in hand; how crossed, the
   instruments;   80
Who wrought with them; and all things else, that
   might
To half a soul, and to a notion crazed,
Say, "Thus did Banquo".

1 MURDERER   You made it known to us.

3.1 A room in the palace

Convincing the Murderers that Banquo has been their enemy, Macbeth asks them what kind of men they are if they are willing to put up with it.

Activities

Character review: Macbeth (11) and the Murderers

In groups of three, re-read the conversation between Macbeth and the Murderers. Then improvise a conversation between the two Murderers in which they explain to a third Murderer (perhaps the one who appears in 3.3) what they plan to do and why they are prepared to do it. The third Murderer might ask questions such as:

- Why do you think it is a good thing to kill Banquo? What have you got against him? (See lines 75–90)
- How did Macbeth go about persuading you? (85–102)
- Why do you think Macbeth spent time persuading you to kill Banquo, when he could have ordered you to do it?
- Why does Macbeth want Banquo killed? (106–107; 115–117)
- Why can't Macbeth do his own dirty work? (117–125)
- How will you go about it? (127–131)
- Why does Fleance have to die as well? (131–137)

87 **so gospelled . . .?** such good Christians . . .?

88 **issue** descendants

90 **beggared yours** made beggars of your children

91–95 **in the catalogue . . .** In the general list of living creatures, you are classed as men; just as **hounds** (etc.) and rough-haired mongrels (**Shoughs** etc.) are all called (**clept**) 'dog'. But the list which puts them in rank order (**file**) distinguishes between . . .

95 **subtle** clever

96 **housekeeper** domestic watchdog

98–99 **whereby . . .** and in that rank order he is given a special quality (**Particular addition**)

101–102 **station in the file . . .** If you think you have a place in the rank order which is not at the bottom, tell me.

103–107 **And I will put . . .** And I will secretly (**in your bosoms**) reveal a plan which will remove (**takes . . . off**) your enemy and make you my closest friends (**Grapples . . .**), because although my health is poor while he is alive, it would be perfect if he were dead.

112–113 **I would set my life . . .** I would take any gamble with my life, to improve it or be rid of it altogether.

MACBETH   I did so; and went further, which is now
                Our point of second meeting. Do you find   85
                Your patience so predominant in your nature
                That you can let this go? Are you so gospelled
                To pray for this good man, and for his issue,
                Whose heavy hand hath bowed you to the grave
                And beggared yours for ever?

1 MURDERER   We are men, my liege. 90

MACBETH   Ay, in the catalogue ye go for men;
                As hounds and greyhounds, mongrels, spaniels, curs,
                Shoughs, water-rugs, and demi-wolves are clept
                All by the name of dogs: the valued file
                Distinguishes the swift, the slow, the subtle,   95
                The housekeeper, the hunter, every one
                According to the gift which bounteous nature
                Hath in him closed; whereby he does receive
                Particular addition, from the bill
                That writes them all alike; and so of men.   100
                Now, if you have a station in the file,
                Not i' the worst rank of manhood, say it;
                And I will put that business in your bosoms,
                Whose execution takes your enemy off,
                Grapples you to the heart and love of us,   105
                Who wear our health but sickly in his life,
                Which in his death were perfect.

2 MURDERER   I am one, my liege,
                Whom the vile blows and buffets of the world
                Have so incensed, that I am reckless what
                I do to spite the world.

1 MURDERER   And I another,   110
                So weary with disasters, tugged with fortune,
                That I would set my life on any chance
                To mend it or be rid on 't.

MACBETH   Both of you
                Know Banquo was your enemy.

BOTH   True, my lord.
MURDERERS

3.1   A room in the palace

Explaining why he cannot simply have Banquo executed, Macbeth convinces the Murderers that Fleance has to die too.

115–117   **distance** (1) argument; or (2) the space between fencers (see **thrusts**, line 116).

118–119   **with bare-faced power ...** as king, I could eliminate him openly, and simply say that it was my wish (**bid my will avouch it**)

121–122   **Whose loves ...** whose support I cannot afford to lose; instead I have to grieve over the death (**wail his fall**) of someone I have killed myself

124–125   **Masking ...** hiding the affair from the public (**the common eye**) for a variety of important (**sundry weighty**) reasons

127   **Your spirits ...** I can see what kind of men you are. *(Macbeth interrupts the first Murderer.)*

129   **Acquaint you ...** Let you know the best time to do the murder.

131–132   **always thought ...** and keep in mind that I must remain free of suspicion

133   **To leave no rubs ...** to keep things tidy

135   **Whose absence ...** whose death is no less important to me

137   **Resolve yourselves apart** Go away and make up your minds.

| MACBETH | So is he mine; and in such bloody distance | 115 |

MACBETH　So is he mine; and in such bloody distance　　115
　　　　　That every minute of his being thrusts
　　　　　Against my near'st of life; and though I could
　　　　　With bare-faced power sweep him from my sight,
　　　　　And bid my will avouch it, yet I must not,
　　　　　For certain friends, that are both his and mine,　120
　　　　　Whose loves I may not drop, but wail his fall
　　　　　Who I myself struck down: and thence it is
　　　　　That I to your assistance do make love,
　　　　　Masking the business from the common eye,
　　　　　For sundry weighty reasons.

2 MURDERER　　　　　　　　　　We shall, my lord,　125
　　　　　Perform what you command us.

1 MURDERER　　　　　　　　　　　　Though our lives –

MACBETH　Your spirits shine through you. Within this hour at
　　　　　　　most
　　　　　I will advise you where to plant yourselves,
　　　　　Acquaint you with the perfect spy o' the time,
　　　　　The moment on 't, for 't must be done tonight　130
　　　　　And something from the palace; always thought
　　　　　That I require a clearness: and with him
　　　　　(To leave no rubs, nor botches, in the work),
　　　　　Fleance his son, that keeps him company,
　　　　　Whose absence is no less material to me　　135
　　　　　Than is his father's, must embrace the fate
　　　　　Of that dark hour. Resolve yourselves apart;
　　　　　I'll come to you anon.

2 MURDERER　　　　　　　　　We are resolved, my lord.

MACBETH　I'll call upon you straight: abide within. –

Exeunt MURDERERS.

　　　　　It is concluded: Banquo, thy soul's flight,　140
　　　　　If it find heaven, must find it out tonight.

Exit.

3.2 A room in the palace

Lady Macbeth reflects that, although they have got what they want, they are not happy, and Macbeth feels that there are still dangers threatening them.

Activities

Character review: Lady Macbeth (5)

Sinéad Cusack thought that Lady Macbeth is bewildered in this scene: 'She's saying, "I've got everything I wanted for him, and he's got everything he ever wanted, but we have no contentment. *Why?*" She doesn't understand.

Do you agree with her?

1. Re-read Lady Macbeth's brief soliloquy (lines 4–7) and discuss: (a) what her state of mind seems to be; (b) how the use of antithesis helps to reflect it (Nought – all; had – spent; desire – without content; destruction – joy).

2. The actress also recalled that, 'In rehearsal we discussed endlessly whether she knew Macbeth was going to kill Banquo, and we came to the conclusion that indeed she did, and she didn't want him to do it . . .' Look carefully at the dialogue and discuss whether or not you support this interpretation: (a) How do you interpret her response in line 38, for example? (b) What is she likely to understand by Macbeth's promise of a 'deed of dreadful note' (44)? (c) Or his reassurance (45–50)? (d) What does she do to make Macbeth say 'Thou marvellest at my words' (54)?

3–4 I would attend ... I would like a few words with him if it is convenient.

4–5 Nought's had ... we have achieved nothing and have given everything, if we are not happy with what we have got

7 Than by destruction ... than to kill someone and then have our happiness ruined by worries

9–11 Of sorriest fancies ... keeping company with depressing thoughts which ought to have died at the same time as the person you are thinking about

11–12 Things without ... If you can't put something right, don't dwell on it.

13 scotched wounded

14–15 She'll close ... She will heal and be herself again, while our feeble attempts at violence (**poor malice**) are in danger from her original venom (**former tooth**). *(The threat has been temporarily removed but will return, more dangerous than before.)*

16–17 But let the frame ... Let the universe fall apart, heaven and earth (**both the worlds**), before (**Ere**) we will ...

20 peace heaven

22 restless ecstasy sleepless delirium

23 fitful restless, subject to fits *(Shakespeare's invention)*

24 nor ... nor ... neither ... nor ...

Scene 2

The same. Another room.

Enter LADY MACBETH and a SERVANT.

LADY
MACBETH

Is Banquo gone from court?

SERVANT

Ay, Madam, but returns again tonight.

LADY
MACBETH

Say to the king, I would attend his leisure
For a few words.

SERVANT

　　　　　　　　　　Madam, I will.

　　　　　　　　　　　　　　　　　　　　　Exit.

LADY
MACBETH

　　　　　　　　　　　Nought's had, all's spent,
Where our desire is got without content:　　　5
'T is safer to be that which we destroy,
Than by destruction dwell in doubtful joy.

Enter MACBETH.

How now, my lord? Why do you keep alone,
Of sorriest fancies your companions making,
Using those thoughts which should indeed have
　　died　　　　　　　　　　　　　　　　　10
With them they think on? Things without all
　　remedy
Should be without regard: what's done is done.

MACBETH

We have scotched the snake, not killed it:
She'll close and be herself; whilst our poor malice
Remains in danger of her former tooth.　　　15
But let the frame of things disjoint, both the worlds
　　suffer,
Ere we will eat our meal in fear, and sleep
In the affliction of these terrible dreams
That shake us nightly. Better be with the dead
Whom we, to gain our place, have sent to peace,　20
Than on the torture of the mind to lie
In restless ecstasy. Duncan is in his grave;
After life's fitful fever he sleeps well;
Treason has done his worst: nor steel, nor poison,

3.2 A room in the palace

*Macbeth expresses his fears concerning Banquo and Fleance and hints
that something terrible is about to happen.*

Activities

Shakespeare's language: visualising the scene

With no scenery or special effects, Shakespeare creates the pictures he needs with words, whereas film versions of the plays are able to produce impressive images. Draw storyboards to show what camera shots might accompany the following sequences in a film of *Macbeth*, in order to create the appropriate atmosphere:

- 40–43 ('Ere the bat . . . night's yawning peal . . .')
- 50–53 ('light thickens . . . do rouse').

In each case, write notes to explain what kind of atmosphere you are aiming for.

25 **Malice domestic** trouble in his own country

levy armies

27 **sleek o'er** smooth over

30 **Let your remembrance . . .** remember to pay special attention to Banquo

31 **Present him . . .** give him special honour

32–35 **Unsafe the while . . .** The present time is so unsafe for us that we have to wash (**lave**) our titles in flattery and use our faces as masks (**vizards**) to hide our true feelings.

38 **in them nature's . . .** (1) they don't hold an everlasting lease on life; (2) their physical bodies will not last for ever

41 **cloistered** *Bats fly through cloisters in old churches.*

42 **shard-borne** born in dung

43 **night's yawning peal** *The beetle's hum is like the tolling of the curfew-bell, rung when people are tired (**yawning**).*

45 **chuck** *a term of affection:* 'chicken'

46 **seeling** blinding *(a falcon's eyes were 'seeled' in training by having the eyelids sewn together)*

49 **Cancel . . .** *Macbeth thinks of Banquo's life as a legal document to be torn up.*

53 **. . . do rouse** they get out of bed to seek their prey

Malice domestic, foreign levy, nothing   25
Can touch him further.

LADY   Come on;
  MACBETH   Gentle my lord, sleek o'er your rugged looks;
Be bright and jovial among your guests tonight.

MACBETH   So shall I, love; and so, I pray, be you.
Let your remembrance apply to Banquo: 30
Present him eminence, both with eye and tongue:
Unsafe the while, that we
Must lave our honours in these flattering streams,
And make our faces vizards to our hearts,
Disguising what they are.

LADY   You must leave this.   35
  MACBETH

MACBETH   O! full of scorpions is my mind, dear wife!
Thou know'st that Banquo and his Fleance lives.

LADY   But in them nature's copy's not eterne.
  MACBETH

MACBETH   There's comfort yet; they are assailable:
Then be thou jocund. Ere the bat hath flown   40
His cloistered flight; ere to black Hecate's summons
The shard-borne beetle, with his drowsy hums,
Hath rung night's yawning peal, there shall be done
A deed of dreadful note.

LADY   What's to be done?
  MACBETH

MACBETH   Be innocent of the knowledge, dearest chuck,   45
Till thou applaud the deed. Come, seeling Night,
Scarf up the tender eye of pitiful day,
And, with thy bloody and invisible hand,
Cancel, and tear to pieces, that great bond
Which keeps me pale! – light thickens; and the
    crow   50
Makes wing to the rooky wood;
Good things of day begin to droop and drowse,
Whiles night's black agents to their preys do rouse.

3.3 A road leading to the palace

The two Murderers waiting to ambush Banquo and Fleance are joined by a third, sent by Macbeth.

Activities

Actors' interpretations (17): the third Murderer

There has been much debate over who the third Murderer is. Discuss each of the following possibilities, grading them from 1 (very unlikely) to 5 (very likely). The third Murderer is:

(a) the 'perfect spy' referred to by Macbeth in the earlier scene (3.1.129), who has given them their final instructions;

(b) Macbeth himself, disguised, checking that the job is properly carried out;

(c) the servant or attendant who announces the Murderers in 3.1;

(d) Rosse (see page 66);

(e) the devil;

(f) a supernatural figure representing Fate or Destiny;

(g) someone sent by Macbeth because he does not trust the two Murderers he has employed.

Keep a note of your gradings for the follow-up to this activity on page 90.

54 **Thou marvellest** you are amazed

55 **Things bad begun ...** enterprises which start off with evil are reinforced by more evil

2–4 **He needs not ...** We don't need to have doubts about him *(the third Murderer)*: he tells us what to do (**delivers Our offices**), exactly according to Macbeth's instructions (**direction just**).

5 **yet** still

6–7 **Now spurs ...** the delayed traveller spurs his horse to get to the inn on time

8 **The subject of our watch** the man we are looking out for

10 **within the note ...** on the list of expected guests at the banquet

11 **go about** are taking the long way round *(with grooms, while Banquo and Fleance are walking)*

Thou marvellest at my words: but hold thee still,
Things bad begun make strong themselves by ill.　　55
So, pr'ythee, go with me.

Exeunt.

Scene 3

The same. A park, with a road leading to the palace.

Enter three MURDERERS.

1 MURDERER　But who did bid thee join with us?

3 MURDERER　　　　　　　　　　　　Macbeth.

2 MURDERER　He needs not our mistrust, since he delivers
Our offices, and what we have to do,
To the direction just.

1 MURDERER　　　　　　　　Then stand with us.
The west yet glimmers with some streaks of day:　　5
Now spurs the lated traveller apace,
To gain the timely inn; and near approaches
The subject of our watch.

3 MURDERER　　　　　　　　Hark, I hear horses.

BANQUO　(*Within*) Give us a light there, ho!

2 MURDERER　　　　　　　　　　Then 't is he; the rest
That are within the note of expectation　　　10
Already are i' the court.

1 MURDERER　　　　　　　His horses go about.

3 MURDERER　Almost a mile, but he does usually,
So all men do, from hence to the palace gate
Make it their walk.

Enter BANQUO, and FLEANCE, with a torch.

2 MURDERER　　　　　　　A light, a light!

3 MURDERER　　　　　　　　　　'T is he.

3.4   A room in the palace

The Murderers kill Banquo but Fleance manages to escape. In the castle, Macbeth welcomes the thanes to the banquet.

Activities

Actors' interpretations (18): the murder of Banquo

The killing of Banquo is a dramatic moment and can be very effective on stage. Block out the movements and then rehearse the scene, trying it first in slow motion, then faster, and finally in realistic time. Pay attention to the details of the script and acting decisions that have to be made:

- How does Fleance contrive to escape?
- Why does the first Murderer strike out the light?
- How do they react to the discovery that Fleance has got away?

Actors' interpretations (19): staging the banquet

Scenes in which people sit around a table can be difficult to stage, because some characters can end up with their backs to the audience, and can also block the audience's view of other characters.

1. Draw a stage plan or a sketch (see the outlines on page 198), to show how you would design this scene, bearing in mind the following factors:
- there are four named characters, plus 'lords'

(Continued on page 88)

15   **Stand to 't** get ready

16   **Let it come down** Let it 'rain' blows.

18   *FLEANCE **escapes** This is one of the major turning points of the play.*

19   **Was 't not the way?** Wasn't that the right thing to do?

20   **but one down** only one killed

1   **degrees** ranks *(they will sit at table in order of rank, from **first** to **last**)*

3   **society** the company

5–6   **Our hostess** will remain seated (**keeps her state**) but I will ask her to welcome you at the appropriate time (**in best time**).

1 MURDERER   Stand to 't.   15

BANQUO   (*To* FLEANCE) It will be rain tonight.

1 MURDERER   Let it come down.

The FIRST MURDERER *strikes out the light while the others assault* BANQUO.

BANQUO   O, treachery! Fly, good Fleance, fly, fly, fly!
Thou mayest revenge – (*To the* MURDERER) O slave!

Dies. FLEANCE *escapes.*

3 MURDERER   Who did strike out the light?

1 MURDERER   Was 't not the way?

3 MURDERER   There's but one down: the son is fled.

2 MURDERER   We have lost   20
Best half of our affair.

1 MURDERER   Well, let's away, and say how much is done.

Exeunt.

Scene 4

A room of state in the palace. A banquet prepared.

*Enter MACBETH, LADY MACBETH, ROSSE, LENOX, LORDS and
attendants.*

MACBETH   You know your own degrees, sit down: at first and
      last,
The hearty welcome.

LORDS   Thanks to your majesty.

MACBETH   Ourself will mingle with society,
And play the humble host.
Our hostess keeps her state, but in best time   5
We will require her welcome.

LADY   Pronounce it for me, Sir, to all our friends;
MACBETH   For my heart speaks, they are welcome.

3.4 A room in the palace

The first Murderer informs Macbeth privately that Banquo has been killed, but Macbeth is dismayed to hear of Fleance's excape.

Activities

- everybody has to have a seat at the banqueting table
- Macbeth has to talk with the Murderers and not be overheard by the lords
- the seat left for Macbeth has to be very visible to the audience
- Banquo's ghost has to be able to enter and exit easily, taking the place left for Macbeth.

2. Macbeth and Lady Macbeth are playing the part of genial host and hostess here (1–12).

(a) Discuss the frequency of the word 'welcome' and its position in the speeches.

(b) Act out the scene, overdoing Macbeth's words of hospitality and finding actions to match.

(c) Find a way for Macbeth to switch easily from addressing the company at large (12 '. . . The table round') to addressing the Murderer privately.

11–12 **Be large in mirth . . .** Enjoy yourselves; in a minute I will drink a toast and pass the cup round.

14 **'T is better thee without . . .** the blood is better *on* you than *in* him

15 **despatched** killed, 'sent off'

19 **. . . the nonpareil** you are without equal

21 **fit** fit of anxiety

   else otherwise

22 **founded** solid and secure, immovable

23 **As broad . . .** as free and unrestrained as the air which surrounds us

24 **cabined, cribbed . . .** *All four expressions mean 'confined, hemmed in, imprisoned'.*

25 **saucy** insolent, *and therefore* nagging

   safe dealt with *(ironic: see the following line)*

27 **trenchèd** cut like trenches

28 **The least . . .** the smallest of which would have been enough to kill him

29–31 Banquo (**the grown serpent**) is dead; but Fleance (**the worm, that's fled**) has it in him to become dangerous, even if he is harmless at present (**No teeth for the present**).

32 **We'll hear ourselves again** We'll discuss this (listen to each other) again tomorrow.

Enter FIRST MURDERER to the door.

MACBETH　(*To* LADY MACBETH) See, they encounter thee with their
　　　　　hearts' thanks.
　　　　　(*To the company*) Both sides are even: here I'll sit i'
　　　　　the midst.　　　　　　　　　　　　　　　　10
　　　　　Be large in mirth; anon, we'll drink a measure
　　　　　The table round. (*To the* MURDERER) There's blood
　　　　　upon thy face.

MURDERER　'T is Banquo's then.

MACBETH　'T is better thee without, than he within.
　　　　　Is he despatched?　　　　　　　　　　　15

MURDERER　My lord, his throat is cut; that I did for him.

MACBETH　Thou art the best o' the cut-throats; yet he's good
　　　　　That did the like for Fleance: if thou didst it,
　　　　　Thou art the nonpareil.

MURDERER　　　　　　　　　　Most royal Sir,
　　　　　Fleance is 'scaped.　　　　　　　　　　20

MACBETH　(*Aside*) Then comes my fit again: I had else been
　　　　　perfect;
　　　　　Whole as the marble, founded as the rock,
　　　　　As broad and general as the casing air:
　　　　　But now I am cabined, cribbed, confined, bound in
　　　　　To saucy doubts and fears. – (*To the* MURDERER) But
　　　　　Banquo's safe?　　　　　　　　　　　25

MURDERER　Ay, my good lord, safe in a ditch he bides,
　　　　　With twenty trenchèd gashes on his head,
　　　　　The least a death to nature.

MACBETH　　　　　　　　　　Thanks for that. –
　　　　　(*Aside*) There the grown serpent lies: the worm, that's
　　　　　fled,
　　　　　Hath nature that in time will venom breed,　　30
　　　　　No teeth for the present. – (*To the* MURDERER) Get
　　　　　thee gone; tomorrow
　　　　　We'll hear ourselves again.

Exit MURDERER.

3.4 A room in the palace

Macbeth pretends to be disappointed at Banquo's absence from the feast and is then appalled at the sight of his ghost.

Activities

Actors' interpretations (20): the Murderers

When Ian McKellen played Macbeth with the Royal Shakespeare Company in 1976, he smiled broadly throughout the opening part of the scene, but when he received the news that Fleance had escaped, his smile became fixed and terrifying.

1. Act out the exchange between Macbeth and the Murderer (12–32), paying attention to the way in which the news of Fleance's escape is broken to Macbeth and to his reaction to it.

2. How does Macbeth's reaction affect your decisions about the identity of the third Murderer (see the activity on page 84)? Why does it make suggestion (b) impossible, and some of the others less likely?

---

33 **give the cheer** behave like a cheery host

33–37 **the feast is sold ...** If you don't keep on telling people that they are welcome, they feel as though they have paid for their meal. They might as well stay at home if they just want to eat; away from home (**From thence**), it is ceremony that makes a meal special; it is empty without it.

37 **Sweet remembrancer!** You have reminded me so sweetly!

40–41 **Here had we now ...** We would have all the greatest nobles here if Banquo were present.

42–43 **Who may I rather ...** Let's hope that he is to be reproached for bad manners, rather than pitied for some accident.

43–44 **His absence ...** He has broken his promise by not being here.

49 **... done this?** Which of you has played this trick on me?

51 **gory locks** bloody hair

| LADY MACBETH | My royal lord, You do not give the cheer: the feast is sold That is not often vouched, while 't is a-making, 'T is given with welcome. To feed were best at home: From thence, the sauce to meat is ceremony; Meeting were bare without it. | 35 |

MACBETH Sweet remembrancer! –
Now, good digestion wait on appetite,
And health on both!

LENOX May it please your highness sit?

MACBETH Here had we now our country's honour roofed, 40
Were the graced person of our Banquo present;

The GHOST OF BANQUO enters, and sits in MACBETH's place.

Who may I rather challenge for unkindness,
Than pity for mischance!

ROSSE His absence, Sir,
Lays blame upon his promise. Please 't your
highness
To grace us with your royal company? 45

MACBETH The table's full.

LENOX Here is a place reserved, Sir.

MACBETH Where?

LENOX Here, my good lord. (*MACBETH notices the* GHOST)
What is 't that moves your highness?

MACBETH Which of you have done this?

LORDS What, my good lord?

MACBETH (*To the* GHOST) Thou canst not say I did it. Never
shake 50
Thy gory locks at me.

ROSSE Gentlemen, rise; his highness is not well.

91

3.4   A room in the palace

Lady Macbeth tries to reassure the thanes that her husband's strange behaviour is nothing to worry about and then privately rebukes him for showing his fear.

Activities

Actors' interpretations (21): the Ghost

In the 1982 Royal Shakespeare Company production, when Macbeth was played by Bob Peck, the ghost was a hallucination. In other words, instead of Banquo entering, covered in blood, Macbeth looked upon an empty chair – which Lady Macbeth (Sara Kestelman) then sat upon to prove that there was nothing there.

1. Discuss whether, if you were the director, you would let the audience see Banquo's ghost or play it as something in Macbeth's mind:
   - What are the advantages and disadvantages in practical terms? Think about the difficulties of staging the scene.
   - What do we lose if the audience is not allowed to see the ghost? What, on the other hand, might be gained?
   - Does it change the meaning of the play, or our attitude to Macbeth, if the ghost is a hallucination?
2. The other thanes do not see the ghost: how should they react?

---

53   **thus** like this

55   **upon a thought** in a moment

56–57   **If much you note him ...** If you stare at him, you will offend him and prolong the fit (**extend his passion**).

60   **O proper stuff!** Rubbish!

61   **painting ...** Your fear is causing you to imagine this.

62   **air-drawn** (1) imaginary; (2) drawn through the air

63–66   **these flaws and starts** These sudden outbursts of emotion – fake compared with genuine fear – (**Impostors ...**) would suit a woman's ghost story, told on the authority of (**Authorised by**) her grandmother.

71–73   **If charnel-houses ...** If buildings where bones are piled, and graves, are going to send back dead bodies, we will have to throw them out for carrion birds to eat.

73   **maws** stomachs

    unmanned in folly Has your foolishness made you lose your manhood completely?

76   **Ere humane statute ...** before human laws cleansed (**purged**) society (**the ... weal**) and made it civilised

78   **the time has been** it used to be the case

LADY **MACBETH**	Sit, worthy friends. My lord is often thus, And hath been from his youth: pray you, keep seat; The fit is momentary; upon a thought 55 He will again be well. If much you note him You shall offend him, and extend his passion; Feed, and regard him not. – (*To* MACBETH) Are you a man?
MACBETH	Ay, and a bold one, that dare look on that Which might appal the devil.
LADY **MACBETH**	O proper stuff! 60 This is the very painting of your fear: This is the air-drawn dagger which, you said, Led you to Duncan. O! these flaws and starts (Impostors to true fear) would well become A woman's story at a winter's fire, 65 Authorised by her grandam. Shame itself! Why do you make such faces? When all's done, You look but on a stool.

MACBETH	(*To the* LORDS) Pr'ythee, see there! behold! look! lo!
	    how say you?
	Why, what care I? (*To the* GHOST) If thou canst nod,
	    speak too. – 70
	(*To the* LORDS) If charnel-houses and our graves must
	    send
	Those that we bury back, our monuments
	Shall be the maws of kites.

GHOST disappears.

LADY **MACBETH**	What! quite unmanned in folly?
MACBETH	If I stand here, I saw him.
LADY **MACBETH**	Fie! for shame!
MACBETH	Blood hath been shed ere now, i' th' olden time, 75 Ere humane statute purged the gentle weal; Ay, and since too, murders have been performed Too terrible for the ear: the time has been

A room in the palace

Macbeth apologises to the thanes and tries to regain his composure, but is unnerved by the reappearance of the ghost.

Activities

Character review: Macbeth (13)

1. Look again at Macbeth's reaction to the ghost (47–51, 69–73, 93–96) and discuss what it is that he seems to find so particularly terrifying in the ghost's appearance and behaviour.

2. What clues do those speeches give about how the actor playing Macbeth might react? (Jonathan Pryce seemed to go completely mad when he saw it; as Sinéad Cusack describes it: 'In one of his convulsive gestures, lunging at a spectre no one else could see, Macbeth had pulled the table-cloth off the table. Then he sat stiffly, his thanes having scattered in disarray, trying to repair the damage by smoothing out the table-cloth.')

81 **mortal murders on their crowns** fatal wounds on their heads

82 **push us ...** (1) take up our seats; (2) take over succession to the throne

84 **do lack you** are missing your company

85 **muse** be surprised

86 **infirmity** illness, weakness

93 **Avaunt!** Be gone!

95 **Thou hast no speculation ...** There is no sign of life in your eyes.

97 **a thing of custom** nothing out of the ordinary

101 **Hyrcan** *from Hyrcania, by the Caspian Sea*

102–103 **Take any shape ...** take any form but Banquo's (**that**) and my firm sinews (**nerves**) will never shake

105–106 **If trembling ...** if I then live in fear and trembling, you can call me a feeble creature

That, when the brains were out, the man would die,
And there an end; but now they rise again,   80
With twenty mortal murders on their crowns,
And push us from our stools. This is more strange
Than such a murder is.

LADY   My worthy lord,
MACBETH   Your noble friends do lack you.

MACBETH   (*To* LADY MACBETH) I do forget. –
(*To the* LORDS) Do not muse at me, my most worthy
              friends;   85
I have a strange infirmity, which is nothing
To those that know me. Come, love and health to all;
Then, I'll sit down. – Give me some wine: fill full. –
I drink to the general joy of the whole table,
And to our dear friend Banquo, whom we miss;   90
Would he were here.

                Re-enter GHOST.

                         To all, and him, we thirst,
              And all to all.

LORDS   Our duties, and the pledge.

MACBETH   (*To the* GHOST) Avaunt! and quit my sight! let the earth
              hide thee!
Thy bones are marrowless, thy blood is cold;
Thou hast no speculation in those eyes,   95
Which thou dost glare with.

LADY   (*To the* LORDS) Think of this, good peers,
MACBETH   But as a thing of custom: 't is no other;
Only it spoils the pleasure of the time.

MACBETH   What man dare, I dare:
Approach thou like the rugged Russian bear,   100
The armed rhinoceros, or the Hyrcan tiger;
Take any shape but that, and my firm nerves
Shall never tremble: or, be alive again,
And dare me to the desert with thy sword;
If trembling I inhabit then, protest me   105
The baby of a girl. Hence, horrible shadow!
Unreal mockery, hence! –

3.4 A room in the palace

The thanes depart in disorder, leaving Macbeth to brood upon the uncanny ways in which murders are often revealed. He wonders suspiciously why Macduff had refused to attent the feast.

109 **displaced the mirth** ruined the merriment

110 **With most admired disorder** with this amazing fit of madness

111–112 **overcome us like a summer's cloud ...?** bring sudden depression upon us, without our showing any shock?

112–113 **You make me strange ...** You make me feel a stranger to the brave character that I possess (**owe**: own).

119 **Stand not ...** Don't worry about leaving in order of rank.

123–126 *Macbeth recalls examples of the natural world conspiring to expose the unnatural sin of murder:* gravestones have moved *(to reveal bodies)*; trees have spoken; magpies, crows (**choughs**) and rooks have exposed the most secretive murderer through prophecies (**Augurs**) and by showing connections between events (**understood relations**).

128–129 **How say'st thou ...** What do you think of the fact that Macduff refuses a king's invitation (to attend the feast)?

GHOST disappears.

Why, so; – being gone,
I am a man again. – Pray you, sit still.

LADY
MACBETH
(*To* MACBETH) You have displaced the mirth, broke
   the good meeting,
With most admired disorder.

MACBETH
                              Can such things be,   110
And overcome us like a summer's cloud,
Without our special wonder? You make me strange
Even to the disposition that I owe,
When now I think you can behold such sights,
And keep the natural ruby of your cheeks,   115
When mine is blanched with fear.

ROSSE
                              What sights, my lord?

LADY
MACBETH
(*To the* LORDS) I pray you, speak not; he grows worse
   and worse;
Question enrages him. At once, good night: –
Stand not upon the order of your going,
But go at once.

LENOX
                  Good night, and better health   120
Attend his majesty!

LADY
MACBETH
                  A kind good night to all.

Exeunt LORDS and attendants.

MACBETH
It will have blood, they say, blood will have blood:
Stones have been known to move, and trees to speak;
Augurs, and understood relations, have
By magot-pies and choughs, and rooks, brought
   forth   125
The secret'st man of blood. What is the night?

LADY
MACBETH
Almost at odds with morning, which is which.

MACBETH
How say'st thou, that Macduff denies his person
At our great bidding?

3.5   **A heath**

Macbeth determines to visit the Witches early the next day to learn the worst that might happen, vowing that further bloody deeds will take place. The Witches are rebuked by the witch goddess Hecate for not involving her in their dealings with Macbeth.

Vivien Leigh as Lady Macbeth and Laurence Olivier as Macbeth in 1955

130   **by the way** on the grapevine: *Macbeth has a paid (**fee'd**) informer in every household*

133   **betimes** very early

135   **the worst means** the most evil methods *(witchcraft)*

135–136   **For mine own good ...** I will sacrifice everything else to get what I want.

136–138   **I am in blood ...** *Macbeth compares his situation to crossing a river of blood: he has gone so far that it would be as difficult to go back as to continue to the other side.*

140   **acted ...** *He thinks of himself as having to perform a part in a play before he has learned (**scanned**) the lines.*

141   **the season of all natures** Sleep is like a seasoning or preservative to keep us fresh.

142–143   **My strange ...** My strange self-deception *(imagining Banquo's ghost)* is only the kind of fear experienced by a beginner (**initiate**), who needs to be toughened up by experience.

144   **young in deed** inexperienced *(they are novices in murder)*

2   **beldams** hags

4   **traffic** have dealings

11–13   **wayward son ...** an unreliable follower ... who loves witchcraft purely for what he can get out of it (**for his own ends**)

LADY MACBETH	Did you send to him, Sir?

MACBETH   I hear it by the way; but I will send.   130
There's not a one of them, but in his house
I keep a servant fee'd. I will tomorrow
(And betimes I will) to the weird sisters:
More shall they speak; for now I am bent to know,
By the worst means, the worst. For mine own good 135
All causes shall give way: I am in blood
Stepped in so far, that, should I wade no more,
Returning were as tedious as go o'er.
Strange things I have in head, that will to hand,
Which must be acted, ere they may be scanned.   140

LADY
MACBETH   You lack the season of all natures, sleep.

MACBETH   Come, we'll to sleep. My strange and self-abuse
Is the initiate fear, that wants hard use:
We are yet but young in deed.

Exeunt.

Scene 5

The heath.

Thunder. Enter the THREE WITCHES, meeting HECATE.

I WITCH   Why, how now, Hecate? you look angerly.

HECATE   Have I not reason, beldams as you are,
Saucy, and overbold? How did you dare
To trade and traffic with Macbeth,
In riddles, and affairs of death;   5
And I, the mistress of your charms,
The close contriver of all harms,
Was never called to bear my part,
Or show the glory of our art?
And, which is worse, all you have done   10
Hath been but for a wayward son,
Spiteful and wrathful; who, as others do,
Loves for his own ends, not for you.

3.6 Somewhere in Scotland

Hecate vows to lead Macbeth to his destruction. Lenox voices his suspicions to another lord about Duncan's and Banquo's deaths.

Activities

Character review: the Witches (2) and Hecate

Hecate is a new character: the Witch goddess.

A Re-read Hecate's speech and discuss (a) what her relationship to the Witches is, and why she has visited them; and (b) what you think she should look like, to fit her role here.

B Some people have suggested that this scene is not by Shakespeare, partly because the verse is different, and that it might have been added because the Witches had proved very popular with audiences. Discuss what contribution the scene makes to the play in terms of what it adds to:
- the plot
- the supernatural atmosphere
- our understanding of Macbeth
- our understanding of the Witches and their motivation.

C Discuss what Hecate's words imply about (a) the Witches' power and its limitations; (b) Macbeth's ultimate fate (bearing in mind that 'security' (line 32) means overconfidence).

---

14 **make amends** put things right

15 **Acheron** *in classical mythology, one of the rivers of the underworld*

21 **Unto a dismal ...** intending something disastrous and fatal

24 **a vaporous drop** *People believed that the moon shed drops of powerful (**profound**) foam on to certain plants.*

26 **sleights** tricks

27–29 *Hecate will raise cunning and deceitful spirits (**artificial sprites**), who, by their power to deceive (**illusion**), will lead Macbeth to his destruction (**confusion**).*

30–31 **bear His hopes ...** he will have unrealistic hopes, and be blind to wisdom, religious grace or fear

32 **security** overconfidence

1–2 **My former speeches ...** What I have already said to you simply corresponds with what you have been thinking; it is up to you to draw your own conclusions. *(Lennox is being deliberately evasive and circumspect: under Macbeth's tyranny it is dangerous for people to voice their opinions openly.)*

2–3 **only I say ...** I will only say that things have been carried on in an odd way (**strangely borne**).

4 **pitied of** pitied by

4 **marry** by the Virgin Mary *(a mild oath)*

But make amends now: get you gone,
And at the pit of Acheron   15
Meet me i' the morning: thither he
Will come to know his destiny.
Your vessels and your spells provide,
Your charms, and everything beside.
I am for the air; this night I'll spend   20
Unto a dismal and a fatal end:
Great business must be wrought ere noon.
Upon the corner of the moon
There hangs a vaporous drop profound;
I'll catch it ere it come to ground: 25
And that, distilled by magic sleights,
Shall raise such artificial sprites,
As, by the strength of their illusion,
Shall draw him on to his confusion.
He shall spurn fate, scorn death, and bear   30
His hopes 'bove wisdom, grace and fear;
And you all know, security
Is mortals' chiefest enemy.

Song, within: "Come away, come away," etc.

Hark! I am called: my little spirit, see,
Sits in a foggy cloud, and stays for me.   35

Exit.

I WITCH   Come, let's make haste: she'll soon be back again.

Exeunt.

Scene 6

Somewhere in Scotland.

Enter LENOX and another LORD.

LENOX   My former speeches have but hit your thoughts,
Which can interpret farther: only, I say,
Things have been strangely borne. The gracious
    Duncan
Was pitied of Macbeth: – marry, he was dead; –
And the right-valiant Banquo walked too late;   5

3.6 Somewhere in Scotland

After Lenox's ironic account of events, the lord reports that Malcolm is with the English King, Edward the Confessor, and that Macduff has journeyed there to find support for an attack upon Macbeth.

Activities

Shakespeare's language: irony

The thanes now live in a country where it is dangerous to speak your mind openly. Lenox therefore has to be very careful about how he expresses his concerns, suspicions and fears. To see how Shakespeare has phrased Lenox's speech:

1. Perform Lenox's words making lines 3–20 ('The gracious Duncan ... so should Fleance') as ironic as possible (giving it a sarcastic tone).

2. Divide the speech up between two people, to give the impression that they agree about Macbeth's tyranny, and perform it with constant awareness that 'walls have ears' and an informer might be just around the corner.

8 **cannot want the thought** cannot help thinking

10 **fact** crime

12 **the two delinquents** *the two grooms attending Duncan*

21 **from broad words** because of his outspoken comments

24 **bestows himself** is staying

25 **... holds the due of birth** *Macbeth is withholding from Malcolm the crown which is rightfully his.*

27 **Edward** *the religious* (**pious**) *English King, Edward the Confessor. His kindness* (**grace**) *and goodness are emphasised as a contrast to Macbeth's evil.*

28–29 **That the malevolence ...** The loss of Malcolm's throne has not meant that he has received less respect.

29–31 **Thither Macduff ...** Macduff has also gone there to ask Edward on Malcolm's behalf (**upon his aid**) to rouse up the Earl of Northumberland and his son, Young Siward.

36 **Do faithful homage ...** show our loyalty to the King and receive honours won and enjoyed in freedom

Whom, you may say, if 't please you, Fleance killed,
For Fleance fled. Men must not walk too late.
Who cannot want the thought how monstrous
It was for Malcolm and for Donalbain
To kill their gracious father? damnèd fact!   10
How it did grieve Macbeth! did he not straight,
In pious rage, the two delinquents tear,
That were the slaves of drink, and thralls of sleep?
Was not that nobly done? Ay, and wisely, too;
For 't would have angered any heart alive   15
To hear the men deny 't. So that, I say,
He has borne all things well; and I do think
That, had he Duncan's sons under his key
(As, an 't please Heaven, he shall not), they should
          find
What 't were to kill a father; so should Fleance.   20
But, peace! – for from broad words, and 'cause he
          failed
His presence at the tyrant's feast, I hear
Macduff lives in disgrace. Sir, can you tell
Where he bestows himself?

LORD   The son of Duncan,
From whom this tyrant holds the due of birth,   25
Lives in the English court; and is received
Of the most pious Edward with such grace,
That the malevolence of fortune nothing
Takes from his high respect. Thither Macduff
Is gone to pray the holy king, upon his aid,   30
To wake Northumberland, and warlike Siward;
That, by the help of these (with Him above
To ratify the work), we may again
Give to our tables meat, sleep to our nights,
Free from our feasts and banquets bloody knives,   35
Do faithful homage, and receive free honours,
All which we pine for now. And this report
Hath so exasperate the king that he
Prepares for some attempt of war.

LENOX   Sent he to Macduff?

LORD   He did: and with an absolute "Sir, not I,"   40
The cloudy messenger turns me his back,

3.6 Somewhere in Scotland

Lenox and the lord agree that Macduff would be well advised to stay out of Macbeth's way.

Activities

Actors' interpretations (22): Lenox and the Lord

1. Like the Old Man in 2.4, the Lord in this scene is not named. Re-read the activity on page 62 and discuss Shakespeare's possible reasons for keeping this lord anonymous.

2. Discuss what you think are the main purposes of this scene, grading the following from 1 (not an important purpose) to 5 (a very important purpose):
   (a) to let us know that there are people who oppose Macbeth, believing him to be a murdering tyrant;
   (b) to provide information about characters we met earlier (such as Malcolm and Macduff);
   (c) to introduce characters we will meet later (such as the English King and Siward);
   (d) to underline who is on whose side;
   (e) to let us know about conditions in Scotland;
   (f) to give the actor playing Macbeth a rest;
   (g) to broaden out the story, reminding us that it is not just about Macbeth and Lady Macbeth.

44–45 **Advise him to a caution ...** warn Macduff to be careful, and keep a sensible distance from Macbeth

48–49 **our suffering country ...** our country which is suffering under Macbeth's evil rule

And hums, as who should say, "You'll rue the time
That clogs me with this answer."

LENOX   And that well might
Advise him to a caution, to hold what distance
His wisdom can provide. Some holy angel   45
Fly to the court of England, and unfold
His message ere he come, that a swift blessing
May soon return to this our suffering country
Under a hand accursed!

LORD   I'll send my prayers with him.

Exeunt.

Exam practice

Character review: the relationship between Macbeth (14) and Lady Macbeth (6)

Act 3 scene 4 is the last scene in which we see Macbeth and Lady Macbeth on stage together, according to Shakespeare's script.

A List the main things that have happened to Lady Macbeth since she became queen and discuss what effect they might have had upon her. Look back particularly to 3.4.

B Write Lady Macbeth's thoughts, as she leaves her husband alone after the banquet, and dwells upon the ways in which their relationship seems to have changed since before the murder. In planning your writing, ask yourself the following questions:
- 3.1.42–43: Is Macbeth rejecting his wife's company, as some stage interpretations suggest?
- 3.2.8–11: Has he become isolated and withdrawn from her?
- 3.2.45–46: Why is he not discussing his plans with her?
- 3.4.58, 60–68, 73–74, 109–110: What effect does his reaction to the ghost have upon their relationship?
- 3.4.122–144: Why does she say so little to him after the thanes have departed? She does not respond to his question about Macduff, his proposal to visit the Witches, or his ominous reference to the need to become hardened to bloody deeds.

C Discuss the change in the relationship between Macbeth and Lady Macbeth, from 1.5 to the end of Act 3, thinking about (a) Macbeth's own perspective, as far as it is apparent; and (b) Lady Macbeth's. Then write each character's diary entry, in which they express their thoughts about the ways in which their relationship is changing.

Plot review (3)

Look back through Act 3 and write one or two newspaper headlines for each scene which best sum up the main events.

Character review: Macbeth (15)

Imagine two of the thanes discuss Macbeth's extraordinary behaviour at the banquet (3.4) after they have been dismissed by Lady Macbeth. Improvise their conversation in pairs and then write a script of it. Your response should include comments on:
- the way Macbeth and his wife greeted you on your arrival
- Macbeth's private conversation with a suspicious-looking character
- what happened when Lenox offered Macbeth the reserved place at the table

- Lady Macbeth's excuses for her husband's behaviour and her words to him
- Macbeth's strange words spoken to the empty chair
- what happened when Macbeth toasted Banquo
- the hasty breaking-up of the meeting.

Character review: Lady Macbeth (7)

A Discuss some of the different ways in which Lady Macbeth can react to her husband's behaviour. For example, does she try to cover it up, or does she become angry with him?

Amanda Root as Lady Macbeth in 1988

B This is how Mrs Pritchard, an eighteenth-century Lady Macbeth, reacted to her husband's behaviour on seeing the ghost:

'Mrs Pritchard showed admirable art [skill] in endeavouring to hide Macbeth's frenzy from the observation of the guests ... She smiled on one, whispered to another, and distantly saluted a third; in short she practised every possible artifice [deception] to hide the transaction that passed between her husband and the vision his disturbed imagination had raised. Her reproving and angry looks, which glanced towards Macbeth, at the same time were mixed with marks of inward vexation and uneasiness. When at last, as if unable to support her feelings any longer, she rose from her seat, and seized his arm, and with a whisper of terror said, "Are you a man!" she assumed a look of such anger, indignation and contempt as cannot be surpassed.'

1. Act out the episode (40–58) reacting as Mrs Pritchard did, and discuss how effective it is to play Lady Macbeth in that way.
2. Sinéad Cusack and Jonathan Pryce in 1986 played the moment very differently: they had a terrible row and the thanes reacted by being extremely embarrassed – and suspicious. Act out the scene again, trying it in that way.

C Discuss how you see Lady Macbeth's character and personality at this point (e.g. is she stronger or weaker than her husband?). Based upon your assessment, what kind of behaviour would therefore be fitting here?

107

4.1　A dark cave

The Witches prepare for their meeting with Macbeth by creating a magic brew.

Activities

Actors' interpretations (23): staging the Witches

The stage directions refer to 'A dark cave'; and yet, when Macbeth arrives, he knocks on a locked door (45–47). Draw a sketch to illustrate what you think might be an effective setting for this scene.

The witches in 1996

1　**brinded cat** brindled, tabby cat; *the first Witch's 'familiar' spirit*

2　**hedge-pig** hedgehog; *the second Witch's familiar*

3　**Harpier** *the third Witch's familiar, perhaps like the mythological harpy – a monster with a woman's body and a bird's wings and claws*

10　**Double ...** let the world's toil and trouble be doubled

12　**Fillet of ...** a thin slice of snake from the fens

17　**howlet** young owl

23　**Witches' mummy** *a medicinal powder made from mummified bodies*

　　maw, and gulf stomach and gullet

24　**ravined** full of prey, gluttonous

26　**blaspheming Jew** *In Shakespeare's time there was an irrational hatred of Jews; Christians took the view that Jews swore against God because they did not believe that Jesus was God's son.*

27–28　**slips** *(poisonous)* cuttings from the yew tree, sliced off **(Slivered)** during an *(ill-omened)* eclipse of the moon

29–30　**Turk** and **Tartar ... birth-strangled babe** *like the Jew, all attractive to the Witches because they were not christened*

31　**Ditch-delivered ...** a prostitute's baby, born in a ditch

Act 4

Scene 1

A dark cave. In the middle, a boiling cauldron.

Thunder. Enter the THREE WITCHES.

1 WITCH	Thrice the brinded cat hath mewed.
2 WITCH	Thrice, and once the hedge-pig whined.
3 WITCH	Harpier cries, 't is time, 't is time.

1 WITCH Round about the cauldron go;
In the poisoned entrails throw.   5
Toad, that under cold stone
Days and nights has thirty-one
Sweltered venom, sleeping got,
Boil thou first i' th' charmèd pot.

ALL Double, double, toil and trouble: 10
Fire, burn; and cauldron, bubble.

2 WITCH Fillet of a fenny snake,
In the cauldron boil and bake;
Eye of newt, and toe of frog,
Wool of bat and tongue of dog,   15
Adder's fork, and blind-worm's sting,
Lizard's leg, and howlet's wing,
For a charm of powerful trouble,
Like a hell-broth boil and bubble.

ALL Double, double, toil and trouble: 20
Fire, burn; and cauldron, bubble.

3 WITCH Scale of dragon, tooth of wolf;
Witches' mummy: maw, and gulf,
Of the ravined salt-sea shark;
Root of hemlock, digged i' th' dark;   25
Liver of blaspheming Jew;
Gall of goat, and slips of yew
Slivered in the moon's eclipse;
Nose of Turk, and Tartar's lips;
Finger of birth-strangled babe,   30
Ditch-delivered by a drab,
Make the gruel thick and slab:

4.1   A dark cave

Macbeth arrives and commands the Witches to answer his questions whatever the consequences.

Activities

Shakespeare's language: the Witches' verse

'Double, double, toil and trouble' has become famous, perhaps because of its use of internal rhyme (double – trouble) and very insistent four-beat rhythm.

1. Act out the scene up to line 38, deciding where characters should speak individually and where in chorus. Which actions might suit the words? Can you think of accompanying music?
2. Write some verses in the same style as a curse upon an enemy of your choice (such as an opposing sports team or an unpopular authority figure).
3. Discuss what Shakespeare's choice of ingredients for the Witches' charm reveals about his audience's superstitions concerning animals and certain human beings.

Themes: order (2)

Macbeth's desperate need to hear further prophecies no matter what the consequences is expressed in a series of visions representing chaos and disorder (52–61). Create a collage to reflect the picture of destruction that he envisages.

---

33 **chaudron** entrails

39 **commend your pains** congratulate you on your trouble

48 **secret, black ...** *They practise black magic.*

50 **I conjure you ...** I call upon you, in the name of the magic you practise (**profess**)

52 **Though you ...** even if you have to

53 **yesty** foaming *(like a liquid to which yeast has been added)*

54 **Confound ... navigation** confuse ships

55 **Though bladed corn ...** even though unripe corn be blown flat

57 **slope** bend

59 **nature's germens** the seeds of creation

60 **Even till destruction sicken** until destruction itself is sick *(with overeating). (Macbeth is willing to sacrifice the future of the universe to get his answers.)*

Add thereto a tiger's chaudron,
For th' ingredients of our cauldron.

ALL　　　　　Double, double, toil and trouble:　　　　　　35
　　　　　　Fire, burn; and cauldron, bubble.

2 WITCH　　　Cool it with a baboon's blood:
　　　　　　Then the charm is firm and good.

Enter HECATE.

HECATE　　　O, well done! I commend your pains,
　　　　　　And every one shall share i' th' gains.　　　　40
　　　　　　And now about the cauldron sing,
　　　　　　Like elves and fairies in a ring,
　　　　　　Enchanting all that you put in.

Music and a song, "Black spirits," etc.

2 WITCH　　　By the pricking of my thumbs,
　　　　　　Something wicked this way comes. – (*Knocking*)　45
　　　　　　Open, locks,
　　　　　　Whoever knocks.

Enter MACBETH.

MACBETH　　How now, you secret, black and midnight hags!
　　　　　　What is 't you do?

ALL　　　　　　　　　　　A deed without a name.

MACBETH　　I conjure you, by that which you profess,　　　50
　　　　　　Howe'er you come to know it, answer me:
　　　　　　Though you untie the winds, and let them fight
　　　　　　Against the churches, though the yesty waves
　　　　　　Confound and swallow navigation up;
　　　　　　Though bladed corn be lodged, and trees blown
　　　　　　　　down;　　　　　　　　　　　　　　　55
　　　　　　Though castles topple on their warders' heads;
　　　　　　Though palaces and pyramids do slope
　　　　　　Their heads to their foundations; though the treasure
　　　　　　Of nature's germens tumble all together,
　　　　　　Even till destruction sicken, answer me　　　60
　　　　　　To what I ask you.

1 WITCH　　　　　　　　　　Speak.

4.1 A dark cave

The Witches' 'masters' take the form of apparitions. An armoured head warns Macbeth about Macduff but a bloody child reassures him that he cannot be harmed by any man to whom a woman has given birth.

Activities

Character review: the Witches (3)

1. Discuss the advantages and disadvantages, and the particular effects achieved, of:
   - having the Witches played by men (as they were in Shakespeare's time)
   - 'doubling' the Witches with the murderers (as in the 1966 Royal Court production)
   - playing them as comic characters (as they did in some Elizabethan plays)
   - portraying them as filthy and disgusting (as in Polanski's 1972 film)
   - making Hecate contrastingly beautiful (as in the 1978 National Theatre production)
   - making them look like ordinary women (as in the 1982 RSC production)
   - portraying them as believable historical figures practising their craft (as in the 1972 National Theatre production).
2. How might the three witches be presented as individuals? For example, in the 1976 RSC production, there were two older witches and a younger one, who was shown to have the special supernatural gifts on which the other two depended.

63 **our masters** *the spirits which control the Witches and now take the form of apparitions*

65 **nine farrow** litter of nine piglets

66 **gibbet** gallows

68 **Thyself, and office, deftly show** cleverly show yourself, performing your function

73 **caution** warning, advice

74 **harped ... aright** You have guessed my fear correctly.

76 **potent** powerful

80 **none of woman born** no man to whom a woman has given birth

2 WITCH   Demand.

3 WITCH   We'll answer.

1 WITCH   Say, if thou 'dst rather hear it from our mouths,
Or from our masters.

MACBETH   Call 'em; let me see 'em.

1 WITCH   Pour in sow's blood, that hath eaten
Her nine farrow; grease, that's sweaten   65
From the murderer's gibbet, throw
Into the flame.

ALL   Come, high or low,
Thyself, and office, deftly show.

Thunder. First APPARITION, an armed head.

MACBETH   Tell me, thou unknown power, –

1 WITCH   He knows thy thought:
Hear his speech, but say thou nought.   70

1 APPARITION Macbeth! Macbeth! Macbeth! beware Macduff;
Beware the Thane of Fife. – Dismiss me. – Enough.

                                               Descends

MACBETH   Whate'er thou art, for thy good caution, thanks:
Thou hast harped my fear aright. But one word
      more:–

1 WITCH   He will not be commanded. Here's another,   75
More potent than the first.

Thunder. Second APPARITION, a bloody child.

2 APPARITION Macbeth! Macbeth! Macbeth! –

MACBETH   Had I three ears, I'd hear thee.

2 APPARITION Be bloody, bold and resolute: laugh to scorn
The power of man, for none of woman born   80
Shall harm Macbeth.

                                               Descends

4.1   A dark cave

Macbeth vows to kill Macduff. Then a third apparition – a child wearing a crown and carrying a tree – tells him that he will not be defeated until Birnam wood comes to Dunsinane.

Activities

Actors' interpretations (24): the apparitions

The apparitions can make a powerful dramatic effect on stage. The armed head perhaps represents Macbeth's, cut off after his death at Macduff's hands (see 5.9.20); the bloody child is presumably Macduff, 'untimely ripped' from his mother's womb (5.8.15–16); and the child with a crown on his head and a tree in his hand is the royal Malcolm with a bough from Birnam wood (5.4.4–7).

The show of kings is a procession of the eight Stuart kings of Scotland, the last one being James VI, who became James I of England and was ruling when Shakespeare wrote this play. It is known that James himself saw a production of *Macbeth* and it is possible that the 'glass' was a mirror, held up in front of the King, to show that 'many more' would descend from him (as, in fact, they have).

Discuss whether you think these apparitions would be more effective if represented by actors or by special effects, and, in either case, how their appearance and disappearance could be staged. Sketch what you think each one should look like.

83–84   **make assurance ...** I will make doubly sure *(by relying on 'none of woman born' and killing Macduff anyway),* and will therefore make Fate stick to its contract (**bond**).

87   **issue** child, descendant

88–89   **round And top of sovereignty** the crown and summit of kingship

90   **lion-mettled** courageous as a lion

90–91   **take no care ...** don't worry who is angry (**chafes**) or complains (**frets**) or plots against you

92   **vanquished** defeated

95   **impress the forest** make the forest join the army

96   **bodements** predictions

97   **Rebellious dead** *Banquo and others who have been killed for opposing Macbeth*

99–100   **the lease of nature ...** the full natural lifespan, and give up his breath *(as though paying a debt)* to time and the natural process of dying (**mortal custom**)

101   **art** skill *(of witchcraft)*

MACBETH   Then live, Macduff: what need I fear of thee?
               But yet I'll make assurance double sure,
               And take a bond of fate: thou shalt not live;
               That I may tell pale-hearted Fear it lies,   85
               And sleep in spite of thunder. –

Thunder. Third APPARITION, a child crowned, with a tree in his hand.

                                            What is this,
               That rises like the issue of a king;
               And wears upon his baby brow the round
               And top of sovereignty?

ALL   Listen, but speak not to 't.

3 APPARITION Be lion-mettled, proud, and take no care   90
               Who chafes, who frets, or where conspirers are:
               Macbeth shall never vanquished be, until
               Great Birnam wood to high Dunsinane hill
               Shall come against him.

                                                    Descends

MACBETH   That will never be:
               Who can impress the forest; bid the tree   95
               Unfix his earth-bound root? Sweet bodements! good!
               Rebellious dead, rise never, till the wood
               Of Birnam rise; and our high-placed Macbeth
               Shall live the lease of nature, pay his breath
               To time and mortal custom. – Yet my heart   100
               Throbs to know one thing: tell me (if your art
               Can tell so much), shall Banquo's issue ever
               Reign in this kingdom?

ALL   Seek to know no more.

MACBETH   I will be satisfied: deny me this,
               And an eternal curse fall on you! let me know. –   105
               Why sinks that cauldron? and what noise is this?

Hautboys.

1 WITCH   Show!

2 WITCH   Show!

4.1 A dark cave

At Macbeth's insistence to know whether Banquo's descendants will ever be kings, the Witches show a procession of eight kings with Banquo.

Activities

Plot review (4): the Witches' prophecies

The Witches' equivocating prophecies are of central importance to the plot. To remind yourself of them, re-read 1.3.48–50; 1.3.65–67; 4.1.71–94 and 4.1.124.

A Write a summary of all the prophecies that the Witches have made since the beginning of the play and note how Macbeth has reacted to them.

B Draw an illustrated wall poster based upon the Witches' prophecies and the related apparitions, which can be displayed as an aid to keep them constantly in mind throughout the rest of the play.

C Discuss the connections between the Witches' prophecies and (a) the theme of equivocation; and (b) the theme of appearance and reality.

113 **sear** scorch

116 **Start, eyes!** Jump from your sockets rather than look at this!

117 **crack of doom** dawning of Doomsday *(the Day of Judgement)*

119 **glass** *either a mirror, or a crystal ball, or a 'magic' glass of some kind*

121 *The* **two-fold balls** *represent the orbs carried in the double coronation of King James in Scotland and England; the* **treble sceptres** *are the two used in the English coronation and one in the Scottish.*

123 **blood-boltered** his hair clotted with blood

124 **for his** claiming them as his descendants

127 **sprites** spirits

130 **antic round** strange, grotesque dance

132 **Our duties . . .** We have welcomed him and paid him homage.

133 **pernicious** harmful

134 **Stand aye accursed** be forever cursed

135 **without there!** you outside!

3 WITCH   Show!

ALL   Show his eyes, and grieve his heart;   110
          Come like shadows, so depart.

A show of eight Kings, the last with a glass in his hand:

BANQUO'S GHOST following.

MACBETH   (*To the first King in the show*) Thou art too like the
              spirit of Banquo: down!
          Thy crown does sear mine eye-balls: (*To the second
              King*) and thy hair,
          Thou other gold-bound brow, is like the first: –
          (*To the* WITCHES) A third is like the former: – filthy
              hags!   115
          Why do you show me this? – a fourth? – Start, eyes!
          What! will the line stretch out to th' crack of doom?
          Another yet? – A seventh? – I'll see no more: –
          And yet the eighth appears, who bears a glass
          Which shows me many more; and some I see   120
          That two-fold balls and treble sceptres carry.
          Horrible sight! – Now, I see 't is true;
          For the blood-boltered Banquo smiles upon me,
          And points at them for his. – What! is this so?

1 WITCH   Ay, Sir, all this is so: – but why   125
          Stands Macbeth thus amazèdly?
          Come, sisters, cheer we up his sprites,
          And show the best of our delights.
          I'll charm the air to give a sound,
          While you perform your antic round;   130
          That this great king may kindly say,
          Our duties did his welcome pay.

Music. The WITCHES *dance, and vanish with* HECATE.

MACBETH   Where are they? Gone? – Let this pernicious hour
          Stand aye accursed in the calendar! –
          Come in, without there!

Enter LENOX.

LENOX   What's your grace's will?   135

117

4.1 A dark cave

The Witches disappear and Lenox arrives to report that Macduff has fled to England. Macbeth decides to attack Macduff's castle and kill his family.

Activities

Character review: Macbeth (16)

Re-read Macbeth's aside (144–155) and discuss how well each of the following adjectives describes him at this point in the play, grading them from 1 (not very accurately) to 5 (very accurately) and quoting evidence from the script to support your assessment:
courageous; impulsive; violent; cowardly; superstitious; intelligent; deceitful; practical; frightened.

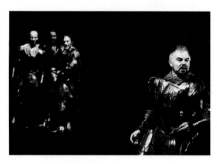

Derek Jacobi as Macbeth in 1993

142   **Macduff is fled ...** *There is immediately truth in the predictions, reinforcing Macbeth's willingness to trust them.*

144–148   **Time, thou anticipat'st ...** Time, you are one step ahead of my terrible actions (**dread exploits**); unless you perform a deed the moment you think of it, it is too late; from now on, I will act as soon as I think.

149   **To crown my thoughts ...** to round off my thoughts with deeds, all within an instant (**be it thought and done**) ...

150–153   *Macbeth instantly decides to attack (**surprise**) Macduff's castle, seize his lands, and kill everyone in his family (**That trace him in his line**).*

154   **before this purpose cool** while I am still fired up to do it

155   **no more sights!** *Macbeth has had enough of apparitions.*

MACBETH	Saw you the weird sisters?
LENOX	No, my lord.
MACBETH	Came they not by you?
LENOX	No, indeed, my lord.

MACBETH Infected be the air whereon they ride;
And damned all those that trust them! – I did hear
The galloping of horse: who was 't came by?   140

LENOX 'T is two or three, my lord, that bring you word,
Macduff is fled to England.

MACBETH   Fled to England?

LENOX Ay, my good lord.

MACBETH (*Aside*) Time, thou anticipat'st my dread exploits:
The flighty purpose never is o'ertook,   145
Unless the deed go with it. From this moment
The very firstlings of my heart shall be
The firstlings of my hand. And even now,
To crown my thoughts with acts, be it thought and
done:
The castle of Macduff I will surprise,   150
Seize upon Fife; give to th' edge o' th' sword
His wife, his babes, and all unfortunate souls
That trace him in his line. No boasting, like a fool;
This deed I'll do, before this purpose cool:
But no more sights! – (*To* LENOX) Where are these
gentlemen?   155
Come, bring me where they are.

Exeunt.

A room in Macduff's castle

Lady Macduff tells Rosse that her husband's flight to England showed little concern for his family.

Activities

Actors' interpretations (25): Rosse

In the Polanski film, Rosse (played by John Stride) is a treacherous figure. He suspects the truth about Duncan's murder when talking to Macduff in 2.4 and goes off to support the tyrant in Scone, where he is seen assisting at the coronation. He acts as the third Murderer and organises the 'disposal' of the other two; and, in this scene, having hypocritically comforted Lady Macduff and her son, he opens the gate to their murderers. After that, he changes sides and takes the news of their death to Macduff in England.

Look back through the play and discuss:
(a) whether there is evidence in the script to support such an interpretation;
(b) whether it makes an interesting interpretation, whether there is evidence for it or not;
(c) what it might add to the play's study of tyranny and its effects.

1   **he** *Macduff*

3–4 **when our actions do not ...** *Even though Macduff was not a traitor, running away made him look like one.*

7   **titles** *lands and possessions owned under the title of Thane of Fife*

9   **He wants the natural touch** He lacks the normal feelings of a father and husband.

12 **All is the fear ...** His actions are motivated totally by fear; not by love for his family.

14 **runs against all reason** goes against common sense

    coz cousin – *a general term for any relative*

15 **school yourself** learn to live with it; control yourself

16 **judicious** possessing sound judgement

17 **The fits o' th' season** the way things violently change these days

18–19 **when we are traitors ...** when we are declared to be traitors, but are not ourselves aware that we are

19–20 **when we hold rumour ...** when we believe rumours, based upon what we fear, but don't know what it is we fear

22 **Each way ...** and are swept this way and that

24 **climb upward** get better

Scene 2

Fife. A room in Macduff's castle.

Enter LADY MACDUFF, her SON and ROSSE.

LADY MACDUFF	What had he done, to make him fly the land?
ROSSE	You must have patience, madam.
LADY MACDUFF	He had none:

His flight was madness: when our actions do not,
Our fears do make us traitors.

ROSSE	You know not

Whether it was his wisdom or his fear.   5

LADY MACDUFF	Wisdom! to leave his wife, to leave his babes,

His mansion, and his titles, in a place
From whence himself does fly? He loves us not;
He wants the natural touch; for the poor wren,
The most diminutive of birds, will fight,   10
Her young ones in her nest, against the owl.
All is the fear, and nothing is the love;
As little is the wisdom, where the flight
So runs against all reason.

ROSSE	My dearest coz,

I pray you, school yourself: but, for your husband,   15
He is noble, wise, judicious, and best knows
The fits o' th' season. I dare not speak much further:
But cruel are the times, when we are traitors,
And do not know ourselves; when we hold rumour
From what we fear, yet know not what we fear,   20
But float upon a wild and violent sea
Each way, and move – I take my leave of you:
Shall not be long but I'll be here again.
Things at the worst will cease, or else climb upward
To what they were before. – (*To her* SON) My, pretty
   cousin,   25
Blessing upon you!

LADY MACDUFF	Fathered he is, and yet he's fatherless.

4.2 A room in Macduff's castle

When Rosse leaves, Lady Macduff's son, who refuses to believe the story that his father is dead, asks about traitors.

Activities

Character review: Lady Macduff

Re-read Lady Macduff's conversation with Rosse and discuss her feelings about her husband's flight. Then write Lady Macduff's diary for the day before, in which she expresses her opinions on:

- conditions in Scotland
- the reasons why her husband might have fled
- what he might hope to achieve in England
- her own safety and that of her children.

Jan Chappell as Lady Macduff in 1996

29 **my disgrace** *Rosse would be embarrassed by weeping.*

30 **dead** as good as dead

34–35 *all kinds of trap for birds:* **lime** sticky bird-lime; **pit-fall** covered hole; **gin** snare

37 **Poor birds ...** Traps are not laid for scrawny birds.

43–44 **Thou speakest ...** You are speaking with all your intelligence; it isn't much, but it's not bad for a child of your age.

48 **swears and lies** takes an oath and breaks it *(Lady Macduff might be thinking of the marriage vows, as well as the oath of loyalty to the King).*

4.2

ROSSE	I am so much a fool, should I stay longer,
	It would be my disgrace and your discomfort:
	I take my leave at once.

Exit.

| LADY MACDUFF | (*To her SON*) Sirrah, your father's dead: | 30 |
| | And what will you do now? How will you live? |

| SON | As birds do, mother. |

| LADY MACDUFF | What, with worms and flies? |

| SON | With what I get, I mean; and so do they. |

| LADY MACDUFF | Poor bird! thou 'dst never fear the net, nor lime, |
| | The pit-fall, nor the gin? | 35 |

SON	Why should I, mother?
	Poor birds they are not set for.
	My father is not dead, for all your saying.

| LADY MACDUFF | Yes, he is dead: how wilt thou do for a father? |

| SON | Nay, how will you do for a husband? | 40 |

| LADY MACDUFF | Why, I can buy me twenty at any market. |

| SON | Then you'll buy 'em to sell again. |

| LADY MACDUFF | Thou speakest with all thy wit; |
| | And yet, i' faith, with wit enough for thee. |

| SON | Was my father a traitor, mother? | 45 |

| LADY MACDUFF | Ay, that he was. |

| SON | What is a traitor? |

| LADY MACDUFF | Why, one that swears and lies. |

4.2 A room in Macduff's castle

A messenger arrives and warns Lady Macduff of approaching danger.

49 **And be all . . .?** And are all people who do that traitors?

57 **enow** enough

61–63 **if you would not, it were . . .** if you don't weep for him, it is a good sign . . . *(because it would show that she hadn't really loved Macduff and is looking for a new husband)*

64 **prattler** chatterbox

66 though I am perfectly acquainted with (**in . . . perfect**) your rank (**your state of honour**)

67 **I doubt . . .** I suspect some danger is very close (**does approach . . .**)

68 **homely** humble, ordinary

69 **hence** get away from here

70–72 **To fright you thus . . .** I know (**methinks**) I am cruel (**savage**) to frighten you in this way; but to harm you (**do worse**) would be terrible (**fell**) cruelty; and that is already too close (**nigh**) to you.

73 **abide** stay

4.2

SON	And be all traitors that do so?
LADY MACDUFF	Every one that does so is a traitor, and must be hanged. 50
SON	And must they all be hanged that swear and lie?
LADY MACDUFF	Every one.
SON	Who must hang them?
LADY MACDUFF	Why, the honest men. 55
SON	Then the liars and swearers are fools; for there are liars and swearers enow to beat the honest men, and hang up them.
LADY MACDUFF	Now God help thee, poor monkey! But how wilt thou do for a father? 60
SON	If he were dead, you 'ld weep for him: if you would not, it were a good sign that I should quickly have a new father.
LADY MACDUFF	Poor prattler, how thou talk'st!

Enter a MESSENGER.

MESSENGER	Bless you, fair dame! I am not to you known, 65
	Though in your state of honour I am perfect.
	I doubt, some danger does approach you nearly:
	If you will take a homely man's advice,
	Be not found here; hence, with your little ones.
	To fright you thus, methinks, I am too savage; 70
	To do worse to you were fell cruelty,
	Which is too nigh your person. Heaven preserve you!
	I dare abide no longer.

Exit.

4.3 England. A room in the King's palace

The Murderers burst in, kill Macduff's son and pursue his fleeing mother. In England, Malcolm is visited by Macduff.

Activities

The murderers killing young Macduff in 1996

Character review: Malcolm (2)

Malcolm is inevitably suspicious of anybody who has come from Scotland, as they might well be agents of Macbeth. Re-read lines 1–28 and list the doubts Malcolm expresses. Then write a letter (in your own words) which Malcolm might just have sent off to his brother Donalbain, in which he voices these doubts about Macduff.

75–77   *In Macbeth's Scotland, doing harm will be praised* (**Is ... laudable**); *doing good is often considered* (**Accounted**) *dangerous foolishness.*

81   **unsanctified** unholy *(and therefore containing devils like the Murderer)*

83   **shag-haired** with shaggy hair *(long and rough)*

83–84   **egg** *and* **fry** *(new-hatched fish) were both terms for small children*

2   **bosoms** *containing the heart, the source of the emotions*

3–4   **Hold fast ...** hold on to the deadly (**mortal**) sword and ... defend the kingdom of our birth *(as though standing over a fallen comrade in battle)*

LADY MACDUFF	Whither should I fly?

LADY
MACDUFF   Whither should I fly?
       I have done no harm. But I remember now
       I am in this earthly world, where to do harm   75
       Is often laudable, to do good sometime
       Accounted dangerous folly: why then, alas,
       Do I put up that womanly defence,
       To say, I have done no harm? What are these faces?

Enter MURDERERS.

MURDERER   Where is your husband?   80

LADY
MACDUFF   I hope, in no place so unsanctified,
       Where such as thou may'st find him.

MURDERER   He's a traitor.

SON   Thou liest, thou shag-haired villain!

MURDERER   What, you egg!

Stabbing him.

       Young fry of treachery!

SON   He has killed me, mother:
       Run away, I pray you!   85

Dies.

Exit LADY MACDUFF, crying "Murder!" and pursued by the MURDERERS.

Scene 3

England. A room in the King's palace.

Enter MALCOLM and MACDUFF.

MALCOLM   Let us seek out some desolate shade, and there
       Weep our sad bosoms empty.

MACDUFF   Let us rather
       Hold fast the mortal sword, and like good men
       Bestride our down-fall birthdom. Each new morn,
       New widows howl, new orphans cry; new sorrows   5

4.3 England. A room in the King's palace

Malcolm is suspicious, fearing that Macduff might betray him to Macbeth for personal reward. Macduff is dismayed to be suspected in this way.

Activities

Character review: Macduff (2)

Re-read 2.4.20–41 and 3.6.29–49. Then hot-seat Macduff (imagining that he has not yet arrived at the English court) and ask him, among other things:

- why he refused to go to Macbeth when asked
- what his plan is in coming to England
- why he left his wife and children unprotected
- what he knows about Malcolm.

6–8 **that it resounds . . .** so that it *(heaven)* echoed as if it felt Scotland's sorrow and screamed out a similar mournful noise

19–20 **. . . may recoil . . .** Someone by nature virtuous might behave wickedly if following orders from the King.

22–24 **Angels . . .** The brightest angel, Lucifer, became a devil (**fell**), but that doesn't mean that all angels are bad; although evil (**foul**) people try to appear good, many others who appear virtuous genuinely are so.

24–25 **. . . my hopes . . . my doubts** *Macduff is losing hope that Malcolm will lead an army against Macbeth; but Malcolm suspects that Macduff might have struck a deal with Macbeth: his family will be protected if Macduff hands over Malcolm.*

27 **motives** people inspiring love

29–30 **Let not my jealousies . . .** I am not suspicious because you have behaved dishonourably, but because I fear for my own safety.

32–34 **. . . lay thou thy basis sure . . .** Tyranny, you can lay secure foundations, because good people are afraid to stop (**check**) you; flaunt your evil deeds openly; Macbeth's title is now legally confirmed (**affeered**)!

Strike heaven on the face, that it resounds
As if it felt with Scotland, and yelled out
Like syllable of dolour.

MALCOLM   What I believe, I'll wail;
What know, believe; and what I can redress,
As I shall find the time to friend, I will.   10
What you have spoke, it may be so, perchance.
This tyrant, whose sole name blisters our tongues,
Was once thought honest: you have loved him well;
He hath not touched you yet. I am young; but
      something
You may deserve of him through me, and wisdom   15
To offer up a weak, poor, innocent lamb,
T' appease an angry god.

MACDUFF   I am not treacherous.

MALCOLM   But Macbeth is.
A good and virtuous nature may recoil
In an imperial charge. But I shall crave your
      pardon: 20
That which you are, my thoughts cannot transpose:
Angels are bright still, though the brightest fell:
Though all things foul would wear the brows of grace,
Yet grace must still look so.

MACDUFF   I have lost my hopes.

MALCOLM   Perchance even there, where I did find my doubts.   25
Why in that rawness left you wife and child
(Those precious motives, those strong knots of love)
Without leave-taking? – I pray you,
Let not my jealousies be your dishonours,
But mine own safeties: you may be rightly just,   30
Whatever I shall think.

MACDUFF   Bleed, bleed, poor country!
Great tyranny, lay thou thy basis sure,
For goodness dare not check thee! wear thou thy
      wrongs;
The title is affeered! – Fare thee well, lord:
I would not be the villain that thou thinkest   35

England. A room in the King's palace

To test Macduff's loyalty, Malcolm pretends to be even more sinful than Macbeth.

39 **sinks beneath the yoke** is dragged down by tyranny

41 **withal** in addition to this

42 **hands uplifted ...** there are people willing to fight on my side

43 **gracious England** *King Edward the Confessor*

48–49 **More suffer ...** My country will suffer more, and in more varied (**sundry**) ways than ever, at the hands of him who succeeds to the throne *(meaning himself)*.

50–52 **in whom I know ...** I know that all the individual vices are so firmly rooted in me, that, when they are revealed (**opened**) ...

55 **confineless harms** boundless evils

57 **to top ...** to beat Macbeth in evils

58 **Luxurious** lustful ... **avaricious** greedy

59 **smacking of** having a 'taste' of

60 **no bottom** no end

61 **voluptuousness** lechery, sexual appetite

62 **matrons ... maids** older and younger women

63–65 **and my desire ...** and my lust would burst through (**o'erbear**) any barriers standing in the way (**continent impediments**) of my sexual desires (**will**)

66–68 **Boundless intemperance ...** Total lack of control is a tyrant; it has caused many a happy reign to come to an early end.

For the whole space that's in the tyrant's grasp,
And the rich East to boot.

MALCOLM   Be not offended:
I speak not as in absolute fear of you.
I think our country sinks beneath the yoke;
It weeps, it bleeds; and each new day a gash   40
Is added to her wounds: I think, withal,
There would be hands uplifted in my right;
And here, from gracious England, have I offer
Of goodly thousands: but, for all this,
When I shall tread upon the tyrant's head,   45
Or wear it on my sword, yet my poor country
Shall have more vices than it had before,
More suffer, and more sundry ways than ever,
By him that shall succeed.

MACDUFF   What should he be?

MALCOLM   It is myself, I mean; in whom I know   50
All the particulars of vice so grafted,
That, when they shall be opened, black Macbeth
Will seem as pure as snow; and the poor state
Esteem him as a lamb, being compared
With my confineless harms.

MACDUFF   Not in the legions   55
Of horrid hell can come a devil more damned
In evils, to top Macbeth.

MALCOLM   I grant him bloody,
Luxurious, avaricious, false, deceitful,
Sudden, malicious, smacking of every sin
That has a name; but there's no bottom, none,   60
In my voluptuousness: your wives, your daughters,
Your matrons and your maids, could not fill up
The cistern of my lust; and my desire
All continent impediments would o'erbear,
That did oppose my will: better Macbeth   65
Than such an one to reign.

MACDUFF   Boundless intemperance
In nature is a tyranny; it hath been
Th' untimely emptying of the happy throne,

4.3 England. A room in the King's palace

Malcolm pretends to be lustful and avaricious and lacking in all the virtues that a king should possess.

70–72   **you may Convey ...** You would be able to enjoy your pleasures secretly while appearing to be chaste (**cold**) – you could deceive (**hoodwink**) people in that way.

73–76   **there cannot be ...** You can't be so lecherous that you would consume all the women who would offer themselves to their king, if he had such desires *(with bawdy allusions to erections in* **greatness** *and* **Finding it so inclined**).

76   **With this** in addition to this

77   **ill-composed affection** character made up of bad qualities

78   **staunchless avarice** insatiable greed; desire for wealth that cannot be satisfied

79   **cut off** kill

80   **... his ... this other's ...** desire one man's jewels, another's house ...

81–82   **my more-having ...** the more I had, the more I would want

82   **forge** invent

84–86   **This avarice ...** This greed is a more serious weakness (**Sticks deeper**), and grows into something much more destructive (**pernicious**) than lust which fades as you grow older.

87   **The sword of ...** Greed is the reason why some kings in the past were murdered.

88–89   **Scotland hath foisons ...** There is wealth enough in Scotland to satisfy your needs, even if you just count your own royal possessions (**your mere own**).

89–90   **All these are ...** All these vices *(lechery, greed, etc.)* are tolerable (**portable**) when set against your virtues (**graces**).

91   **king-becoming graces** virtues which a king ought to have

92–94   **As justice ...** such as justice, truthfulness (**verity**), moderation (**temperance**) ... generosity (**Bounty**) ... humility (**lowliness**), love of God (**Devotion**) ... strength of character (**fortitude**) ...

95–96   I have no trace (**relish**) of good qualities, but I have an abundance of (**abound In**) each feature of every individual (**several**) sin.

98   **concord** peace and harmony

99–100   **Uproar the universal peace ...** throw the peace of the universe into confusion and destroy all world unity

And fall of many kings. But fear not yet
To take upon you what is yours; you may   70
Convey your pleasures in a spacious plenty,
And yet seem cold – the time you may so hoodwink:
We have willing dames enough; there cannot be
That vulture in you, to devour so many
As will to greatness dedicate themselves,   75
Finding it so inclined.

MALCOLM   With this, there grows
In my most ill-composed affection such
A staunchless avarice, that, were I king,
I should cut off the nobles for their lands;
Desire his jewels, and this other's house;   80
And my more-having would be as a sauce
To make me hunger more, that I should forge
Quarrels unjust against the good and loyal,
Destroying them for wealth.

MACDUFF   This avarice
Sticks deeper, grows with more pernicious root   85
Than summer-seeming lust; and it hath been
The sword of our slain kings: yet do not fear;
Scotland hath foisons to fill up your will,
Of your mere own. All these are portable,
With other graces weighed.   90

MALCOLM   But I have none: the king-becoming graces,
As justice, verity, temperance, stableness,
Bounty, perseverance, mercy, lowliness,
Devotion, patience, courage, fortitude,
I have no relish of them; but abound   95
In the division of each several crime,
Acting it many ways. Nay, had I power, I should
Pour the sweet milk of concord into hell,
Uproar the universal peace, confound
All unity on earth.

MACDUFF   O Scotland! Scotland!   100

MALCOLM   If such a one be fit to govern, speak:
I am as I have spoken.

4.3 England. A room in the King's palace

Finally believing that Malcolm is as full of vices as he claims, Macduff angrily rejects him as fit to rule Scotland. This is the reassurance that Malcolm needs and he explains that he had lied about his vices to test Macduff's loyalty.

102 **Fit to govern?** *Malcolm's slandering of himself has finally had the desired effect: by rejecting such an 'evil' man as king, Macduff proves his loyalty.*

104 **untitled** with no legal right to the throne

106 **issue of** heir to

107 **interdiction** accusation of himself *(as being incapable of ruling)*

108 **does blaspheme his breed** slanders his family

111 **Died every day ...** constantly prepared herself for heaven

112 **These evils thou repeat'st ...** (1) the evils you report about yourself; (2) your evils which are the same as Macbeth's

114–117 **Macduff, this noble passion ...** *Macduff's emotional reaction, caused by his honest character (**Child of integrity**), has satisfied Malcolm that he is loyal, wiping out all suspicious doubts (**black scruples**) ...*

118 **trains** tricks, plots

119–120 **and modest wisdom ...** cautious good sense holds me back from believing people too hastily

120–121 **God above ...** may God direct our dealings

122 **I put myself ...** I place myself under your guidance.

123–125 **Unspeak ...** I take back everything I said against myself; deny (**abjure**) the sins and crimes I accused myself of, as things foreign to my nature.

125–128 **I am yet Unknown ...** I am still a virgin, have never lied, have hardly ever been envious of (**coveted**) other people's possessions, never broke a promise

133 **Whither, indeed ...** and it was there *(to Scotland)* that, before your arrival ...

135 **at a point** fully prepared for battle

136 **Now we'll together** Now we'll go there together. *(Malcolm invites Macduff to join in the army led by himself and Old Siward.)*

136–137 **and the chance of goodness ...** may our chance of success be equal to the justice of our cause

138–139 **Such welcome ...** *Macduff finds it hard to process in his mind all the good and bad news he has just heard.*

MACDUFF   Fit to govern?
No, not to live. – O nation miserable!
With an untitled tyrant, bloody-sceptered!
When shalt thou see thy wholesome days again,   105
Since that the truest issue of thy throne
By his own interdiction stands accused,
And does blaspheme his breed? Thy royal father
Was a most sainted king: the queen that bore thee,
Oft'ner upon her knees than on her feet,   110
Died every day she lived. Fare thee well!
These evils thou repeat'st upon thyself
Hath banished me from Scotland. – O my breast,
Thy hope ends here!

MALCOLM   Macduff, this noble passion,
Child of integrity, hath from my soul   115
Wiped the black scruples, reconciled my thoughts
To thy good truth and honour. Devilish Macbeth
By many of these trains hath sought to win me
Into his power, and modest wisdom plucks me
From over-credulous haste: but God above   120
Deal between thee and me! for even now
I put myself to thy direction, and
Unspeak mine own detraction; here abjure
The taints and blames I laid upon myself
For strangers to my nature. I am yet   125
Unknown to woman; never was forsworn;
Scarcely have coveted what was mine own;
At no time broke my faith: would not betray
The devil to his fellow; and delight
No less in truth than life: my first false speaking   130
Was this upon myself. What I am truly
Is thine, and my poor country's, to command:
Whither, indeed, before thy here-approach,
Old Siward, with ten thousand warlike men,
Already at a point, was setting forth.   135
Now we'll together, and the chance of goodness
Be like our warranted quarrel! Why are you silent?

MACDUFF   Such welcome and unwelcome things at once,
'T is hard to reconcile.

Enter a DOCTOR.

4.3 England. A room in the King's palace

As Malcolm explains King Edward the Confessor's powers to cure 'the King's evil', Rosse arrives to report the latest news from Scotland.

Activities

Themes: kingship (1)

The reference to King Edward's curing of 'the evil' and the images of disease elsewhere in the play might be said to reflect evil (which is a disease) and Macbeth himself, the disease from which his country suffers.

A Imagine you are the doctor in King Edward's court. Write a brief letter to a fellow doctor, giving a report on the illness mentioned in this scene and describing how Edward cures it.

(Continued on page 138)

142 **stay his cure** are waiting to be cured by him

142–145 **their malady convinces ...** Their disease defeats the greatest medical skill; but heaven has granted his hand such holy power (**sanctity**) that, at his touch, they instantly recover (**presently amend**).

146 **the evil** *Scrofula was known as 'the King's Evil' because English kings were said to be able to cure it by touching.*

149 **solicits heaven** gets heaven's help

150 **strangely-visited ...** people with strange illnesses *(perhaps 'visited' by evil spirits)*

152 **the mere despair ...** people whom the doctors have completely given up on

153 **stamp** coin

154–156 **and 't is spoken ...** and it is said that he will hand down this blessed power (**benediction**) of healing to the king who succeeds him

156 **With this ...** As well as this strange talent ...

162–163 May God quickly (**betimes**) take away the conditions (**means**) which cause us to be strangers to one another!

164 **Stands Scotland where it did?** Are things still the same in Scotland?

MALCOLM	Well, more anon.
	(*To the* DOCTOR) Comes the king forth, I pray you? 140

DOCTOR Ay, sir; there are a crew of wretched souls
That stay his cure: their malady convinces
The great assay of art; but, at his touch,
Such sanctity hath heaven given his hand,
They presently amend.

MALCOLM   I thank you, doctor.   145

Exit DOCTOR.

MACDUFF What's the disease he means?

MALCOLM   'T is called the evil:
A most miraculous work in this good king,
Which often, since my here-remain in England,
I have seen him do. How he solicits heaven,
Himself best knows; but strangely-visited people,   150
All swoln and ulcerous, pitiful to the eye,
The mere despair of surgery, he cures;
Hanging a golden stamp about their necks,
Put on with holy prayers: and 't is spoken,
To the succeeding royalty he leaves   155
The healing benediction. With this strange virtue
He hath a heavenly gift of prophecy;
And sundry blessings hang about his throne
That speak him full of grace.

Enter ROSSE.

MACDUFF   See, who comes here.

MALCOLM My countryman; but yet I know him not.   160

MACDUFF My ever-gentle cousin, welcome hither.

MALCOLM I know him now. Good God betimes remove
The means that makes us strangers!

ROSSE   Sir, amen.

MACDUFF Stands Scotland where it did?

ROSSE   Alas, poor country!

4.3 England. A room in the King's palace

Rosse reports that Macduff's family are well and that good men are preparing to rebel against Macbeth's tyranny. Malcolm confirms his plans to invade Scotland with the support of an English army.

Activities

B Re-read the account of King Edward's curing and, in pairs, discuss all the contrasts which can be drawn with Macbeth's behaviour and character:

King Edward . . .   whereas Macbeth . . .

- is called 'this good king'   ....
- 'solicits heaven'   ....
- cures the sick   ....
- utters 'holy prayers'   ....
- leaves the power of healing to his heirs   ....
- has the gift of prophecy   ....
- is famed for his virtues   ....

C Both Edward and Duncan are presented as examples of good kings. Re-read Macbeth's comments on Duncan's good qualities (in 1.7.16–20) and look again at Duncan's behaviour in 1.4. Then write about 'Kingship in *Macbeth*', comparing the presentation of the two saintly kings with that of Macbeth himself.

166–167 **where nothing ...** where the only cheerful people are those who know nothing

168–169 **... Are made, not marked** Terrible sounds are uttered, but nobody notices them any more.

170 **modern ecstasy** common emotion

170–171 **the dead man's knell ...** when the funeral bell tolls, people scarcely bother to ask whom it is for

173 **Dying or ere ...** good men's lives end before they have time to fall ill and die naturally

173–174 **O relation ...!** Oh, this report is too elaborate but too true!

175–176 **That of ...** Anyone telling hour-old news will be hissed by their audience *(because they have heard it already)*; each minute gives rise to (**teems**) fresh news.

179 *The expression* **well at peace** *can be a euphemism for 'dead'.*

180 **Be not a niggard ...** Don't be mean with your words

182–185 **ran a rumour ...** There was a rumour going around that many good men were preparing for battle (**out**); and I was more prepared to believe that because I saw Macbeth's army on the march.

186 **eye** appearance

188 **To doff ...** to throw off their terrible miseries

Almost afraid to know itself. It cannot   165
Be called our mother, but our grave; where nothing,
But who knows nothing, is once seen to smile;
Where sighs, and groans, and shrieks that rend the air
Are made, not marked; where violent sorrow seems
A modern ecstasy: the dead man's knell   170
Is there scarce asked for who; and good men's lives
Expire before the flowers in their caps,
Dying or ere they sicken.

MACDUFF   O relation
Too nice and yet too true!

MALCOLM   What's the newest grief?

ROSSE   That of an hour's age doth hiss the speaker;   175
Each minute teems a new one.

MACDUFF   How does my wife?

ROSSE   Why, well.

MACDUFF   And all my children?

ROSSE   Well, too.

MACDUFF   The tyrant has not battered at their peace?

ROSSE   No; they were well at peace when I did leave 'em.

MACDUFF   Be not a niggard of your speech: how goes 't?   180

ROSSE   When I came hither to transport the tidings,
Which I have heavily borne, there ran a rumour
Of many worthy fellows that were out;
Which was, to my belief, witnessed the rather,
For that I saw the tyrant's power afoot.   185
Now is the time of help. Your eye in Scotland
Would create soldiers, make our women fight
To doff their dire distresses.

MALCOLM   Be 't their comfort,
We are coming thither. Gracious England hath
Lent us good Siward, and ten thousand men;   190

4.3 England. A room in the King's palace

Rosse breaks the news to Macduff about the murder of his wife and children.

Activities

Actors' interpretations (27): Rosse breaking the news

1. Look back at the activity on page 120, which explored the different ways in which the character of Rosse can be interpreted. Then act out his breaking of the news to Macduff in two different ways: first as though he is a genuine friend; then as a person who until recently had been one of Macbeth's right-hand men.

2. Discuss which of the two approaches you prefer, in terms of how it fits your interpretation of the scene and the play as a whole.

3. Finally, annotate the scene (or make notes on a separate piece of paper), bearing in mind your preferred interpretation, to help the actor playing Rosse convey the right emotions and attitudes. Mark in, giving advice on:
   • movements and actions
   • where to pause
   • how to speak the lines (e.g. shouting, whispering)
   • facial expression
   • how the character is feeling (upset, nervous, etc.).

192 **gives out** can boast of

192–193 **Would I could ...** I wish I could respond to this comforting news with something similar.

195 **latch** catch

195–197 **What concern they ...?** Is this bad news for everybody or does it apply to one particular person? (**fee-grief Due to** – *legal language: a grief owned by a single person*)

199 **Pertains to** belongs to

202 **possess them with** inform them precisely with

204 **is surprised** has been taken by surprise

205–207 **to relate ...** If I were to report the way in which they were killed, I would add your death to theirs. (*Notice the 'deer'/'dear' pun*).

206 **quarry** *heap of animals killed in hunting*

208 **ne'er pull your hat ...** *Perhaps Macduff does not literally do this (a traditional sign of grief), but hides his face in his hands.*

210 **Whispers ...** whispers to the overstressed heart and persuades it to break

212 **And I must be from thence!** And I had to be away from home!

An older and a better soldier none
That Christendom gives out.

ROSSE   Would I could answer
This comfort with the like! But I have words
That would be howled out in the desert air,
Where hearing should not latch them.

MACDUFF   What concern they? 195
The general cause? or is it a fee-grief
Due to some single breast?

ROSSE   No mind that's honest
But in it shares some woe, though the main part
Pertains to you alone.

MACDUFF   If it be mine,
Keep it not from me; quickly let me have it.   200

ROSSE   Let not your ears despise my tongue for ever,
Which shall possess them with the heaviest sound
That ever yet they heard.

MACDUFF   Humph! I guess at it.

ROSSE   Your castle is surprised; your wife and babes
Savagely slaughtered: to relate the manner   205
Were, on the quarry of these murdered deer,
To add the death of you.

MALCOLM   Merciful heaven! –
What, man! ne'er pull your hat upon your brows:
Give sorrow words; the grief that does not speak
Whispers the o'er-fraught heart, and bids it break.   210

MACDUFF   My children too?

ROSSE   Wife, children, servants, all
That could be found.

MACDUFF   And I must be from thence!
My wife killed too?

ROSSE   I have said.

MALCOLM   Be comforted:

4.3 England. A room in the King's palace

Malcolm tried to comfort Macduff over the loss of his family. They leave to prepare for the invasion of Scotland.

Activities

Actors' interpretations (28): 'He has no children'

There are at least three possible interpretations of Macduff's response 'He has no children' (216). He could be referring to:

- Malcolm, accusing him of not understanding his grief
- Macbeth, who would not have had Macduff's children killed if he had himself been a father
- Macbeth, on whom he cannot take an appropriate revenge, by killing his children.

Act out the exchange (213–216) in three different ways, trying to reflect the three interpretations. Then discuss which of the three you prefer: in particular, which fits your overall interpretation of Macduff?

217–219 **hell-kite** *Macbeth attacked Macduff's* **chickens** *and their* **dam** *(mother) like a bird of prey from hell, in one deadly* (**fell**) *swoop.*

223–226 **Sinful Macduff!** ... *Macduff feels guilty and worthless* (**Naught**) *that his family have been killed because of his sins, rather than through any faults* (**demerits**) *of their own.*

231 **Cut short all intermission** let there be no interval *(between now and his confrontation with Macbeth)*

231 **front to front** face to face

233–234 **if he 'scape** ... If he escapes, it will only be because I have forgiven him; in which case, may heaven forgive him as well.

234 **This time goes manly** that's a man's reaction

236 **Our lack is nothing** ... All that remains for us to do is leave.

237 **ripe for shaking** like ripe fruit ready to be shaken from the tree

237–238 **and the powers above** ... and the heavenly powers are arming themselves

239 **The night is long** ... It is a long night that has no dawn. *(However bad things are, they will come to an end at some time.)*

	Let's make us medicines of our great revenge,	
	To cure this deadly grief.	215

MACDUFF
He has no children. – All my pretty ones?
Did you say all? – O hell-kite! – All?
What, all my pretty chickens, and their dam,
At one fell swoop?

MALCOLM   Dispute it like a man.

MACDUFF   I shall do so;
But I must also feel it as a man: 220
I cannot but remember such things were,
That were most precious to me. – Did heaven look on,
And would not take their part? Sinful Macduff!
They were all struck for thee. Naught that I am,
Not for their own demerits, but for mine   225
Fell slaughter on their souls: heaven rest them now!

MALCOLM
Be this the whetstone of your sword: let grief
Convert to anger; blunt not the heart, enrage it.

MACDUFF
O! I could play the woman with mine eyes,
And braggart with my tongue. – But, gentle
    heavens,   230
Cut short all intermission; front to front
Bring thou this fiend of Scotland and myself;
Within my sword's length set him; if he 'scape,
Heaven forgive him too!

MALCOLM   This time goes manly,
Come, go we to the King: our power is ready;   235
Our lack is nothing but our leave. Macbeth
Is ripe for shaking, and the powers above
Put on their instruments. Receive what cheer you may;
The night is long that never finds the day.

Exeunt.

Exam practice

Themes: kingship (2)

Throughout many of Shakespeare's plays, there is an exploration of what makes a good king.

A Imagine that you are a contemporary of Shakespeare's and discuss the qualities which, in your opinion, would make a good king. In pairs, put into your own words the qualities that Malcolm describes himself as possessing in 4.3.125–131. Then discuss how important you think these qualities might have been for a good king in Shakespeare's time.

B Study the qualities listed in lines 92–94 and discuss which of them:
(a) were apparent in Duncan;
(b) are obviously not found in Macbeth;
(c) are still to be seen in some form in Macbeth, but have now been perverted.

C Write about Shakespeare's exploration of kingship and what makes a good king in *Macbeth*. Refer in detail to what you have learned about the character and behaviour of (a) Duncan; (b) Macbeth; (c) Edward the Confessor; and (d) Malcolm (as the king-to-be).

Character review: Malcolm (3)

Look back through 4.3. Then write a second letter from Malcolm to his brother Donalbain, in which he recounts the conversation with Macduff and explains his plans. You could write about:
- his initial suspicions of Macduff (1–44)
- his testing of Macduff's loyalty (44–114)
- his reaction to Macduff's responses (114–139)
- Rosse's news about Macbeth and the state of Scotland (164–185)
- Macduff's reaction to the news of his family's slaughter (193–234)
- future plans (189–192 and 235–239).

Plot review (5)

As the final Act is about to begin, it is important to understand exactly where the major characters are and what they are planning to do. The map opposite shows where some of the characters are at the end of Act 4 (most of the Scottish thanes have been placed in their home areas). Look back through Act 4:

1. Sketch out a rough copy of the map, adding the following, according to where they were at the end of Act 4: Macbeth, Macduff, Rosse, Malcolm,

Donalbain, Siward (Earl of Northumberland – see 4.3.190–192).
2. Add notes to show what main things might be going through some of their
   minds at this point in the story. For example:
   • What is Macbeth feeling (a) after hearing the latest prophecies (4.1); (b)
     knowing that people are beginning to rebel against him (4.3)?
   • What things are going through Macduff's head (4.3)?
   • What are Malcolm's plans (4.3)?

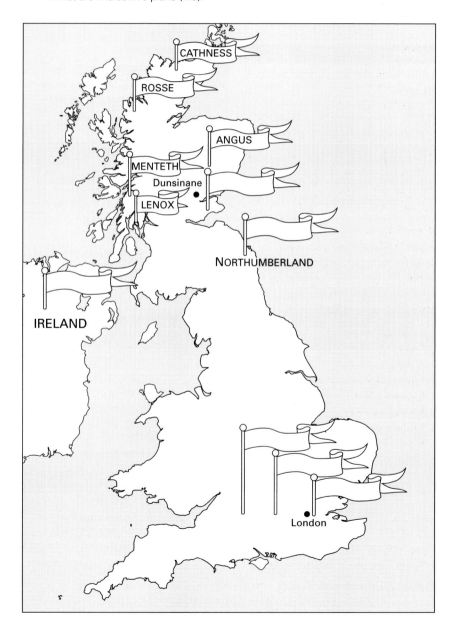

Dunsinane – a room in the castle

Lady Macbeth's gentlewoman tells a doctor about her mistress's behaviour while sleepwalking. Then she appears, asleep and carrying a candle.

Activities	

Actors' interpretations (29): directing the scene

Sinéad Cusack gives a detailed account of her actions in this scene when she played Lady Macbeth:

'I was very *busy* in my sleep, and I found that a great help, coming down fast, in the sleepwalking scene . . . I felt that her particular brand of unrest would be those frantic little devil-thoughts that you can't knock out of your mind . . . about blood, about *blood* . . . and that's certainly the way the sleepwalking speech is written – erratic, disjointed.'

1. Annotate the scene to provide advice to the actress playing the part and then act it out in groups of three. Give advice on:
   • movements and actions
   • how to speak the lines
   • where to pause
   • facial expressions
   • how the character is feeling and why.

(Continued on page 148)

1 **watched** kept watch

4 **went into the field** led his army into battle

5 **night-gown** dressing-gown

6 **closet** *private chest for valuables*

10–12 **perturbation in nature . . .** disorder in her mind and body, to be able to gain the benefit of sleep while at the same time (**at once**) behave as though awake

12 **slumbery agitation** sleepwalking

13 **actual performances** things you have actually seen her do

16 **most meet** extremely fitting and proper

17–18 **having no witness . . .** *The gentlewoman is afraid she will be accused of inventing the extraordinary report she could give.*

taper *candle*

19 **Lo you!** . . . Look! . . . This is the way she behaved before (**her very guise**).

20–21 **stand close** keep out of sight

23–24 *Lady Macbeth now* **has light by her continually** *because she is terrified of the dark.*

26 **their sense are shut** Her eyes are open but she is not actually seeing anything.

Act 5

Scene 1

Dunsinane. A room in the castle.

Enter a DOCTOR OF PHYSIC and a WAITING-GENTLEWOMAN.

DOCTOR   I have two nights watched with you, but can
perceive no truth in your report. When was it she
last walked?

GENTLE-   Since his majesty went into the field, I have seen
WOMAN   her rise from her bed, throw her night-gown   5
upon her, unlock her closet, take forth paper, fold
it, write upon 't, read it, afterwards seal it, and
again return to bed; yet all this while in a most
fast sleep.

DOCTOR   A great perturbation in nature, to receive at once   10
the benefit of sleep, and do the effects of
watching! In this slumbery agitation, besides her
walking and other actual performances, what, at
any time, have you heard her say?

GENTLE-   That, Sir, which I will not report after her.   15
WOMAN

DOCTOR   You may to me; and 't is most meet you should.

GENTLE-   Neither to you, nor any one, having no witness to
WOMAN   confirm my speech.

Enter LADY MACBETH, with a taper.

Lo you! here she comes. This is her very guise,
and, upon my life, fast asleep. Observe her: stand   20
close.

DOCTOR   How came she by that light?

GENTLE-   Why, it stood by her: she has light by her
WOMAN   continually; 't is her command.

DOCTOR   You see, her eyes are open.   25

GENTLE-   Ay, but their sense are shut.
WOMAN

147

5.1 Dunsinane – a room in the castle

In her sleepwalking Lady Macbeth imagines she is washing blood off her hands and talks about the murders that have taken place.

Activities

2. Imagine making a film in which, instead of portraying the sleepwalking, the screen showed what was going on in Lady Macbeth's head. List the nightmare visions in her mind, noting how each one is connected to a line that she utters, and sketch out three or four frames of the storyboard.

Cheryl Campbell as Lady Macbeth in 1993

Character review: Lady Macbeth (8)

Discuss how far it is possible to find evidence in the script of each of the following qualities in Lady Macbeth: toughness; ruthlessness; deceitfulness; intelligence; ambition; dominance; a willingness to use evil supernatural agencies. What other qualities do you see in her?

32 **Yet** still *(she cannot get her hands clean: there is still a spot of blood remaining)*

33 **set down** write down

34 **satisfy my remembrance** back up my memory

36–37 **One; two ...** *She imagines she hears the bell telling them* **'t is time to do 't** *(the murder: see 2.1.62).*

38 **afeard** afraid

39–40 **when none can call our power to account** when we are so powerful that nobody can make us account for our actions

42 **Do you mark that?** *(Shocked:)* Did you hear that?

44 **will these hands ne'er be clean?** *We might recall Lady Macbeth's confidence that 'A little water clears us of this deed': 2.2.64.*

45–46 **mar all ...** ruin everything with your nervousness (**starting**)

47 **Go to** *a common expression when someone is shocked by something (he is not telling the gentlewoman to go away)*

53 **sorely charged** carrying a heavy burden *(of guilt and torment)*

55 **dignity** worth, value

DOCTOR	What is it she does now? Look, how she rubs her hands.
GENTLE-WOMAN	It is an accustomed action with her, to seem thus washing her hands. I have known her continue in this a quarter of an hour. 30
LADY MACBETH	Yet here's a spot.
DOCTOR	Hark! she speaks. I will set down what comes from her, to satisfy my remembrance the more strongly. 35
LADY MACBETH	Out, damned spot! out, I say! – One; two; why, then 't is time to do 't. – Hell is murky. – Fie, my Lord, fie! a soldier, and afeard? – What need we fear who knows it, when none can call our power to account? – Yet who would have thought the 40 old man to have had so much blood in him?
DOCTOR	Do you mark that?
LADY MACBETH	The Thane of Fife had a wife: where is she now? – What, will these hands ne'er be clean? – No more o' that, my lord, no more o' that: you mar all 45 with this starting.
DOCTOR	Go to, go to: you have known what you should not.
GENTLE-WOMAN	She has spoke what she should not, I am sure of that: heaven knows what she has known.
LADY MACBETH	Here's the smell of the blood still: all the 50 perfumes of Arabia will not sweeten this little hand. Oh! oh! oh!
DOCTOR	What a sigh is there! The heart is sorely charged.
GENTLE-WOMAN	I would not have such a heart in my bosom for the dignity of the whole body. 55
DOCTOR	Well, well, well –
GENTLE-WOMAN	Pray God it be, sir.

5.1 Dunsinane – a room in the castle

The doctor leaves, shocked at what he has seen and heard.

Activities

Character review: Lady Macbeth (9)

A According to Lady Macbeth's actions and speeches in this scene, what particular events (rather than just the general reaction to the murder of Duncan) seem to have disturbed her mind?

B The gentlewoman talks of Lady Macbeth taking paper and writing on it. Discuss what the letter might contain. Could it be, for example:
- a letter to Macbeth, perhaps asking why he no longer confides in her?
- a confession?
- a letter warning Lady Macduff?

Decide what seems to you to be most in keeping with her character and then draft the letter.

C Write the doctor's confidential report on Lady Macbeth, including an account of her symptoms and his secret fears about what her words imply.

58 **beyond my practice** beyond my skill as a doctor

63 **on's** of his

64 **Even so?** Is that the way things are? *(The doctor understands the reference to Banquo.)*

67 **What's done cannot be undone** Remember: 'what's done is done' (3.2.12).

69 **Will she ...** The emphasis is on 'Will'.

70 **Directly** immediately

71 **Foul whisp'rings are abroad** There are ugly rumours going around.

71–72 **Unnatural deeds** *(murdering a king – Duncan)* **Do breed unnatural troubles** *(rebelling against a king – Macbeth)*

73 **discharge** confide, reveal

74 **More needs she ...** She has more need of a priest than a doctor.

76 **means of all annoyance** anything that she might harm herself with *(he fears she will attempt suicide)*

78 **mated** bewildered

DOCTOR	This disease is beyond my practice: yet I have known those which have walked in their sleep, who have died holily in their beds.

60

LADY MACBETH	Wash your hands, put on your night-gown; look not so pale. – I tell you yet again, Banquo's buried: he cannot come out on's grave.

DOCTOR	Even so?

LADY MACBETH	To bed, to bed: there's knocking at the gate. Come, come, come, come, give me your hand. What's done cannot be undone. To bed, to bed, to bed.

65

Exit.

DOCTOR	Will she go now to bed?

GENTLE-WOMAN	Directly.

70

DOCTOR	Foul whisp'rings are abroad. Unnatural deeds Do breed unnatural troubles: infected minds To their deaf pillows will discharge their secrets. More needs she the divine than the physician. – God, God forgive us all! Look after her; Remove from her the means of all annoyance, And still keep eyes upon her. – So, good-night: My mind she has mated, and amazed my sight. I think, but dare not speak.

75

GENTLE-WOMAN	Good-night, good doctor.

Exeunt.

5.2 The country near Dunsinane

The Scottish army opposing Macbeth approaches Dunsinane and the thanes discuss Macbeth's loss of control.

Activities

Plot review (6): the approaching battle

Copy the sketch map below and add the names of (a) the Scottish thanes approaching Dunsinane; and (b) the English army led by Siward, with Malcolm and Macduff. Where do you think the Witches ought to be placed?

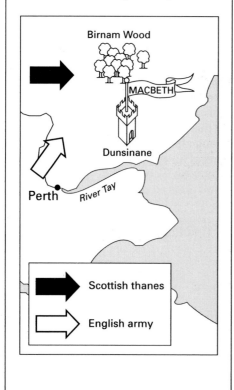

Birnam Wood

MACBETH

Dunsinane

Perth River Tay

➡ Scottish thanes

⇨ English army

colours regimental banners and flags

3–5 **Revenges burn in them ...** Malcolm and Macduff are burning with the desire for revenge, for their grievous wrongs (**dear causes**) would be enough to raise a dead (**mortified**) man to an enthusiasm for the bloodshed and din of battle (**alarm**).

6 **well** in all probability

8 **file** list

10 **unrough** unbearded *(therefore: young)*

11 **Protest their first ...** proclaim that they are now for the first time acting like men

15–16 **He cannot buckle ...** *Like a man with dropsy* (**distemper**), *who cannot fasten his belt around his swollen body, Macbeth is unable to control the tyrannically ruled kingdom.*

18–20 **Now minutely ...** Every minute rebellions rebuke (**upbraid**) him for his disloyalty (**faith-breach**) (to Duncan); people obey him because they are following orders – not out of love.

20–22 **now does he feel ...** *Macbeth has become a pathetic figure unsuited to the great title of king.*

22–25 **Who then shall blame ...?** Who can blame Macbeth's troubled nerves for being jumpy, when his whole nature revolts against his existence?

Scene 2

The country near Dunsinane.

Enter, with drums and colours, MENTETH, CATHNESS,
ANGUS, LENOX and soldiers.

MENTETH The English power is near, led on by Malcolm,
His uncle Siward, and the good Macduff.
Revenges burn in them; for their dear causes
Would, to the bleeding and the grim alarm,
Excite the mortified man.

ANGUS   Near Birnam wood   5
Shall we well meet them: that way are they coming.

CATHNESS Who knows if Donalbain be with his brother?

LENOX For certain, Sir, he is not. I have a file
Of all the gentry: there is Siward's son,
And many unrough youths, that even now   10
Protest their first of manhood.

MENTETH   What does the tyrant?

CATHNESS Great Dunsinane he strongly fortifies.
Some say he's mad: others, that lesser hate him,
Do call it valiant fury; but, for certain,
He cannot buckle his distempered cause   15
Within the belt of rule.

ANGUS   Now does he feel
His secret murders sticking on his hands;
Now minutely revolts upbraid his faith-breach:
Those he commands move only in command,
Nothing in love: now does he feel his title   20
Hang loose about him, like a giant's robe
Upon a dwarfish thief.

MENTETH   Who then shall blame
His pestered senses to recoil and start,
When all that is within him does condemn
Itself for being there?

CATHNESS   Well; march we on,   25

5.3 Dunsinane – a room in the castle

As the rebel Scots march towards Birnam to meet the English army led by Malcolm and Macduff, Macbeth receives reports of the approaching forces, but comforts himself with the Witches' predictions.

Activities

Character review: Macbeth (18)

A Macbeth quotes two of the prophecies which give him a feeling of security (2–6). In pairs, look back at 4.1 to check that you can remember what the prophecies were, and give your opinions on which ones will make Macbeth feel confident and which ones will give him cause for concern.

B In groups, write some of the reports which Macbeth seems to have been receiving (referred to in line 1), starting with events which follow the meeting between Malcolm, Macduff and Rosse in England (4.3). They will presumably contain news of (a) the thanes who are deserting him ('let them fly all'); (b) the alliances formed against him; and (c) day-by-day bulletins of the armies' approach. As a sequence, the reports should give a summary of what has been happening since the end of Act 4. Each group writes one report and then annotates it with comments and reactions in Macbeth's handwriting.

(Continued on page 156)

27–29 **Meet we the medicine ...** Just as men purge their illnesses by bloodletting, so we will meet the doctor to this diseased country (**sickly weal**) and with him we will pour out the last drop of our blood in battle.

30 **To dew** to water

sovereign (1) royal; (2) having power as medicine

3 **taint** become weak with (*as a vegetable goes rotten*)

5 **All mortal consequences** everything that will happen to human beings

8 **epicures** *The hardy Scot, Macbeth, despises the English for their soft-living.*

9 **... sway by** the mind I rule myself by

11 **damn thee black** *Damned souls, and the devil, were believed to be black.*

cream-faced loon ... idiot, white with fear; *compare:* 15 **lily-livered** (*lacking red-blooded courage*); 16 **linen** (*bleached*) **cheeks**; 17 **whey-face** (*whey is the thin liquid left over from curdled milk*)

14 **Go, prick thy face ...** smear your face with red blood to cover the paleness

15 **patch** clown, fool

16–17 **those linen cheeks ...** your white cheeks persuade others to be afraid

To give obedience where 't is truly owed:
Meet we the medicine of the sickly weal;
And with him pour we, in our country's purge,
Each drop of us.

LENOX   Or so much as it needs
To dew the sovereign flower and drown the weeds.   30
Make we our march towards Birnam.

Exeunt, marching.

Scene 3

Dunsinane, a room in the castle.

Enter MACBETH, DOCTOR and attendants.

MACBETH   Bring me no more reports: let them fly all:
Till Birnam wood remove to Dunsinane
I cannot taint with fear. What's the boy Malcolm?
Was he not born of woman? The spirits that know
All mortal consequences have pronounced me
      thus: 5
"Fear not, Macbeth; no man that's born of woman
Shall e'er have power upon thee." – Then fly, false
      thanes,
And mingle with the English epicures:
The mind I sway by, and the heart I bear,
Shall never sag with doubt, nor shake with fear.   10

Enter a SERVANT.

The devil damn thee black, thou cream-faced loon!
Where gott'st thou that goose look?

SERVANT   There is ten thousand –

MACBETH   Geese, villain?

SERVANT   Soldiers, sir.

MACBETH   Go, prick thy face, and over-red thy fear,
Thou lily-livered boy. What soldiers, patch?   15
Death of thy soul! those linen cheeks of thine
Are counsellors to fear. What soldiers, whey-face?

5.3 Dunsinane – a room in the castle

Macbeth faces the fact that he cannot look forward to an old age of comfort and respect. The doctor reports that Lady Macbeth's sickness is of the mind.

Activities

1. In some classical drama, the tragic hero displays *hubris* – an unreasonable self-confidence – before his final fall. Discuss Macbeth's show of hubris in the beginning of 5.3 (1–17). Consider:
   - his confidence in the prophecies
   - his attitude to the English
   - his own courage
   - his treatment of the frightened servant.

   How does this behaviour make the audience feel about Macbeth?

2. After the show of hubris, Macbeth calls for Seyton. Discuss what he might be about to say when he breaks off to call Seyton again: 'I am sick at heart, When I behold – ' (19–20) Behold what?

Character review: Lady Macbeth (10)

Look back at the activity involving the doctor's confidential report (page 150) and add the brief additional comment which he writes up after this conversation with Macbeth (37–46), drawing conclusions about 'troubles of the brain' and how they can, or cannot, be cured.

19 The **Seyton** *family were hereditary armour-bearers to the kings of Scotland.*

20 **push** attack

21 **disseat me** throw me off my throne

22–23 **... Is fall'n into the sere ...** *Just as a plant becomes withered and yellow with age, so the course (**way**) of Macbeth's life has entered its final stage.*

25 **As** such as

26 **I must not look to have** I cannot expect

27 **mouth-honour** *People say flattering things because of his power, not because they mean them.*

27–28 **breath, Which ...** words which are mere air, and which the speaker would prefer to deny, but does not dare to

35 **skirr** scour, rush through

37–39 **Not so sick ...** It is not that she is sick; rather that she is disturbed by persistent hallucinations which prevent her from sleeping.

40 **minister to** treat as a doctor

42 **Raze out** erase

43 **oblivious antidote** medicine which would help her forget

44 **stuffed ...** overfull with tormenting, dangerous thoughts (**perilous stuff**)

SERVANT	The English force, so please you.

MACBETH	Take thy face hence. (*Exit SERVANT*) – Seyton! – I am

                    sick at heart,
When I behold – Seyton, I say! – This push   20
Will cheer me ever, or disseat me now.
I have lived long enough: my way of life
Is fall'n into the sere, the yellow leaf;
And that which should accompany old age,
As honour, love, obedience, troops of friends,   25
I must not look to have; but, in their stead,
Curses, not loud but deep, mouth-honour, breath,
Which the poor heart would fain deny, and dare not.
Seyton!

Enter SEYTON.

SEYTON	What's your gracious pleasure?

MACBETH	What news more? 30

SEYTON	All is confirmed, my lord, which was reported.

MACBETH	I'll fight, till from my bones my flesh be hacked.

         Give me my armour.

SEYTON	'T is not needed yet.

MACBETH	I'll put it on.

         Send out more horses, skirr the country round;   35
Hang those that talk of fear. Give me mine armour. –
(*To the DOCTOR*) How does your patient, doctor?

DOCTOR	Not so sick, my lord,

         As she is troubled with thick-coming fancies,
That keep her from her rest.

MACBETH	Cure her of that:

         Canst thou not minister to a mind diseased,   40
Pluck from the memory a rooted sorrow,
Raze out the written troubles of the brain,
And with some sweet, oblivious antidote
Cleanse the stuffed bosom of that perilous stuff
Which weighs upon the heart?

5.4 The country near Dunsinane

As Macbeth struggles into his armour, the doctor leaves, wishing he were well away from Dunsinane. The two armies opposing Macbeth have joined forces.

Activities

Actors' interpretations (30): arming Macbeth

Act out the lines in which Macbeth is putting his armour on (and taking it off), talking to the doctor and giving orders to Seyton, all at the same time. Use a coat to represent the armour and rehearse the sequence so as to give an idea of the physical movements and urgency with which the scene ends.

Character review: Macbeth (19)

In the speech beginning 'I have lived long enough . . .' (22–28), Macbeth thinks about the things that he might have looked forward to in old age, but can now not expect.

Discuss (a) exactly what these are (e.g. it will help to look back at 1.4.28–29 and 1.7.31–35); (b) what effects the events since Duncan's murder have had on Macbeth and his wife; and (c) whether the speech gives you any sympathy for Macbeth.

45–46 **Therein the patient . . .** that is something for which the patient has to provide his (or her) own treatment

47 **physic** medicine

48 **staff** *carried to show that he is king*

49 **despatch** Get on with it!

50–52 **If thou couldst . . . cast . . .** *Macbeth sees Scotland as a sick person in need of medical attention:* If you could, doctor, analyse (**cast**) my country's urine, find out what disease it is suffering from, and cleanse (**purge**) it to its original (**pristine**) sound health.

55–56 **rhubarb** *and* **senna** *are laxatives* (**purgative drug**) *to clean out the body* (**scour**) *of the English.*

59 **bane** destruction

62 **Profit** financial reward *(the traditional motive of doctors in Shakespeare's time)*

2 **chambers** bedrooms; *he is referring to Duncan's murder:* 'When we can sleep safely in our beds.'

DOCTOR	Therein the patient 45
	Must minister to himself.

MACBETH   Throw physic to the dogs; I'll none of it. –
                (*To* SEYTON) Come, put mine armour on; give me my
                  staff. –
                Seyton, send out. – (*To the* DOCTOR) Doctor, the thanes
                  fly from me. –
                (*To* SEYTON) Come, Sir, despatch. – (*To the* DOCTOR)
                  If thou couldst, doctor, cast 50
                The water of my land, find her disease,
                And purge it to a sound and pristine health,
                I would applaud thee to the very echo,
                That should applaud again. – (*To* SEYTON) Pull't off, I
                  say. –
                (*To the* DOCTOR) What rhubarb, senna, or what
                  purgative drug, 55
                Would scour these English hence? – Hear'st thou of
                  them?

DOCTOR   Ay, my good lord: your royal preparation
                Makes us hear something.

MACBETH   (*To* SEYTON) Bring it after me. –
                I will not be afraid of death and bane
                Till Birnam forest come to Dunsinane. 60

Exit.

DOCTOR   (*Aside*) Were I from Dunsinane away and clear,
                Profit again should hardly draw me here.

Exeunt.

Scene 4

Country near Dunsinane. A wood in view.

*Enter, with drum and colours, MALCOLM, OLD SIWARD and his SON,
MACDUFF, MENTETH, CATHNESS, ANGUS, LENOX, ROSSE, and
SOLDIERS, marching.*

MALCOLM   Cousins, I hope the days are near at hand,
                That chambers will be safe.

5.5 Dunsinane – within the castle

Malcolm orders that every man must cut down a bough from Birnam wood so that they can conceal the army's true size, and reports that many men have deserted from Macbeth.

Activities

Actors' interpretations (31): Birnam wood

Malcolm orders: 'Let every soldier hew him down a bough' (4). Although the script does not imply that this action has to take place on stage, some productions do find ways of showing it, as it can be a dramatic and impressive scene. Give your own ideas about how this famous moment – the cutting down of boughs from the trees in Birnam wood – can be made to work on stage.

4–7 hew him down ... Every soldier is to cut himself a branch and carry it in front of him. In that way we will conceal (**shadow**) the size of our army (**host**) and make people who spy on us (**discovery**) give false reports (**Err**).

10–14 'Tis his main hope ... Fortifying the castle and withstanding a siege is Macbeth's only hope. Followers of all ranks have deserted when they saw an opportunity and those remaining are enforced soldiers whose hearts are not in the fight.

14–16 Let our ... If our judgements (**censures**) are to be accurate (**just**), we had better wait to see what actually happens (**the true event**); we would do best to behave like (**put we on**) good soldiers.

19–21 Thoughts speculative ... Guesswork builds up our hopes; but it is the battle (**strokes**) that decides the actual outcome (**certain issue**). So let the war advance towards that point.

3–4 here let them lie ... They can stay here until eaten up by starvation and fever.

MENTETH	We doubt it nothing.
SIWARD	What wood is this before us?
MENTETH	The wood of Birnam.

MALCOLM   Let every soldier hew him down a bough,
And bear 't before him: thereby shall we shadow   5
The numbers of our host, and make discovery
Err in report of us.

SOLDIERS   It shall be done.

SIWARD   We learn no other but the confident tyrant
Keeps still in Dunsinane, and will endure
Our setting down before 't.

MALCOLM   'T is his main hope;   10
For where there is advantage to be gone,
Both more and less have given him the revolt,
And none serve with him but constrainèd things,
Whose hearts are absent too.

MACDUFF   Let our just censures
Attend the true event, and put we on   15
Industrious soldiership.

SIWARD   The time approaches
That will, with due decision, make us know
What we shall say we have, and what we owe.
Thoughts speculative their unsure hopes relate,
But certain issue strokes must arbitrate;   20
Towards which advance the war.

Exeunt, marching.

Scene 5

Dunsinane. Within the castle.

Enter, with drum and colours, MACBETH, SEYTON and soldiers.

MACBETH   Hang out our banners on the outward walls;
The cry is still, "They come!" Our castle's strength
Will laugh a siege to scorn; here let them lie,

Dunsinane – within the castle

Macbeth boasts that his castle can withstand a siege indefinitely but is disturbed by the cry of women. Hearing that Lady Macbeth is dead, he reflects on the pointlessness of life.

Activities

Shakespeare's language: 'Tomorrow, and tomorrow ...'

This is the most famous speech in the play and is worth learning by heart, so as to internalise it and gain the fullest understanding and feeling of its possible meanings.

A Create a collage, painting or drawing to illustrate one visual image in the soliloquy (such as 'Life's but a walking shadow') and then discuss what the picture adds to your understanding of the story of Macbeth.

5 **forced with those ...** reinforced with people who should be on our side

17 **She should have died hereafter** *either* (1) she ought to have died at some future time; *or* (2) she would have had to die some time or other.

18 **There would have been a time ...** *either* (1) there was a time when I could have responded to such an announcement; *or* (2) the word would have to be spoken at some time; *or* (3) there would have been a better time for such news.

19–21 **Tomorrow ...** Each day follows the next, creeping at this trivial speed (**in this petty pace**) until the last word has been written down in the book of time.

22–23 **And all our yesterdays ...** Every day in past history has done no more than provide light for fools on their journey to death (**dusty** *perhaps recalls 'Dust to dust ...' in the funeral service*).

24–26 **a poor player ...** *Now life is like an actor,* **poor** *because (1) he will not be on stage for long, and (2) he is not very skilled;* he struts around and expresses his unhappiness (**frets**) for a short while **And then is heard no more**.

(Continued on page 164)

Till famine and the ague eat them up.
Were they not forced with those that should be
    ours,   5
We might have met them dareful, beard to beard,
And bear them backward home. (*A cry within, of
women*) What is that noise?

SEYTON   It is the cry of women, my good lord.

                            Exit.

MACBETH   I have almost forgot the taste of fears.
The time has been, my senses would have cooled 10
To hear a night-shriek; and my fell of hair
Would, at a dismal treatise, rouse and stir,
As life were in 't. I have supped full with horrors:
Direness, familiar to my slaughterous thoughts,
Cannot once start me.

Re-enter SEYTON.
                      Wherefore was that cry?   15

SEYTON   The queen, my lord, is dead.

MACBETH   She should have died hereafter:
There would have been a time for such a word. –
Tomorrow, and tomorrow, and tomorrow,
Creeps in this petty pace from day to day,   20
To the last syllable of recorded time;
And all our yesterdays have lighted fools
The way to dusty death. Out, out, brief candle!
Life's but a walking shadow, a poor player
That struts and frets his hour upon the stage,   25
And then is heard no more: it is a tale
Told by an idiot, full of sound and fury,
Signifying nothing.

Enter a MESSENGER.

Thou com'st to use thy tongue; thy story quickly.

MESSENGER   Gracious my lord,   30
I should report that which I say I saw,
But know not how to do 't.

5.6 Dunsinane – outside the castle

A messenger brings news that Birnam wood appears to be moving and Macbeth begins to wonder whether the Witches might have deceived him. Weary of life, he determines to fight to the last. Malcolm gives orders about the attack.

Activities

B To understand some of the many different meanings of the soliloquy and the different ways in which it can be delivered, try saying it:

- as a radio broadcast
- as a prophecy by one of the Witches
- in the tones of an embittered loser
- as an optimistic fatalist
- as someone realising the truth of each line as they utter it.

Discuss which kind of delivery brings out the most interesting and illuminating meanings in terms of your interpretation of the play as a whole, and which reading you think is right for Macbeth as you see him.

C It is perhaps natural that a man of the theatre like Shakespeare should express his feelings about the meaning of life in theatre images (the 'poor player' who 'struts and frets his hour upon the stage'). Draft your own soliloquy to express your feelings about the meaning of life – or some aspect of it – using images appropriate to you and your interests (sport? music? partying?). Try writing the speech in iambic pentameters (see pages 202–203).

34 **anon** suddenly

40 **Till famine cling thee** until you shrivel up from starvation

40–41 **if thy speech be sooth ...** If you are telling the truth, I don't care if you do the same to me.

42–44 **I pull in resolution ...** I can no longer give free rein to my confidence and I begin to question the devil's cunning arguments (**equivocation**; *see 2.3.9–12*) which make lies sound like truth.

47–48 **If this ...** If what he claims (**avouches**) turns out to be true, there is no point in either running away or staying here.

49–50 **I 'gin ...** I am beginning to be tired of life (**the sun**) and wish that the ordered universe (**estate o' th' world**) would fall apart.

51 **wrack** destruction (wreck)

52 **harness** gear, armour. *(Macbeth is determined to die fighting. Had he remained in the castle, he might have outlasted the siege; as it is, by sallying forth and encountering Macduff, he enables the prophecy to be fulfilled.)*

2 **show like those ...** let people see you as you really are

4 **first battle** the main part of the army

MACBETH	Well, say, sir.

MESSENGER As I did stand my watch upon the hill,
I looked toward Birnam, and anon, methought,
The wood began to move.

MACBETH   Liar and slave!   35

MESSENGER Let me endure your wrath, if 't be not so.
Within this three mile may you see it coming;
I say, a moving grove.

MACBETH   If thou speak'st false,
Upon the next tree shalt thou hang alive,
Till famine cling thee: if thy speech be sooth,   40
I care not if thou dost for me as much. –
I pull in resolution, and begin
To doubt th' equivocation of the fiend,
That lies like truth: "Fear not, till Birnam wood
Do come to Dunsinane"; – and now a wood   45
Comes toward Dunsinane. – Arm, arm, and out!
If this which he avouches does appear,
There is nor flying hence, nor tarrying here.
I 'gin to be aweary of the sun,
And wish th' estate o' th' world were now undone.   50
Ring the alarum bell! – Blow, wind! come, wrack!
At least we'll die with harness on our back.

Exeunt.

Scene 6

The same. A plain before the castle.

Enter, with drum and colours, MALCOLM, OLD SIWARD,
MACDUFF, etc., and their army, with boughs.

MALCOLM Now, near enough: your leafy screens throw down,
And show like those you are. – (*To old SIWARD*) you,
   worthy uncle,
Shall, with my cousin, your right noble son,
Lead our first battle: worthy Macduff and we
Shall take upon 's what else remains to do,   5

Dunsinane – outside the castle

In the battle, Macbeth encounters Siward's son, confident that he cannot be harmed by any man born of woman.

Activities

Character review: Macbeth (20)

Discuss the following lines in 5.5 and 5.7 and consider some of Macbeth's feelings and attitudes as he approaches the final moments of his life: 5.5, lines 42–44, 49–50, 51–52; 5.7, lines 1–4.

Miles Anderson as Macbeth in 1986

6   **order** battle strategy

7–8   **Do we but ...** All we ask is to encounter Macbeth's army tonight; then let us fight or be defeated.

10   **clamorous harbingers** noisy announcers

1–2   **They have tied me ...** *Macbeth thinks of himself as a bear, tied to the stake to be baited by dogs, with no alternative but to fight it out.*

2   **the course** a round of bear-baiting

What's he What kind of man can it be

10   **abhorrèd** detested, loathed

11   **I'll prove the lie ...** I'll prove that you are speaking lies.

According to our order.

SIWARD   Fare you well. –
Do we but find the tyrant's power tonight,
Let us be beaten, if we cannot fight.

MACDUFF   Make all our trumpets speak; give them all breath,
Those clamorous harbingers of blood and death.   **10**

Exeunt. Alarms continued.

Scene 7

The same. Another part of the plain.

Enter MACBETH.

MACBETH   They have tied me to a stake: I cannot fly,
But, bear-like, I must fight the course. – What's he
That was not born of woman? Such a one
Am I to fear, or none.

Enter YOUNG SIWARD.

YOUNG
SIWARD   What is thy name?

MACBETH   Thou'lt be afraid to hear it.   **5**

YOUNG
SIWARD   No; though thou call'st thyself a hotter name
Than any is in hell.

MACBETH   My name's Macbeth.

YOUNG
SIWARD   The devil himself could not pronounce a title
More hateful to mine ear.

MACBETH   No, nor more fearful.

YOUNG
SIWARD   Thou liest, abhorrèd tyrant: with my sword   **10**
I'll prove the lie thou speak'st.

5.7 Dunsinane – outside the castle

Macbeth kills Young Siward and exits as Macduff enters, looking for him.
Malcolm and Old Siward enter Macbeth's castle.

Activities

Actors' interpretations (32): the battle

In *Henry V*, Shakespeare was apologetic about the inability of his theatre to give a proper representation of the Battle of Agincourt, and the same applies to any battle in his plays. Use the stage plans and drawings on page 198 to plan out scene 7, noting any use of sound effects, and walk it through in slow motion to see how it works. (The Battle of Agincourt in Kenneth Branagh's film of *Henry V* had an effective slow-motion sequence.)

One technical problem to solve is what to do with Young Siward's body (as Old Siward does not notice it when he enters).

15 **... slain, and with no stroke of mine** If anybody else has killed you

17 **Kernes** *Macbeth has to make up his army with Irish foot soldiers, fighting as mercenaries* (**whose arms Are hired**), *just as the rebel Macdonwald had done (see 1.2.12–13).*

18 **staves** spear-shafts

either thou I will either fight you

20 **undeeded** unused *(without having performed any deeds)*

20–22 **There thou shouldst be ...** That's where you *(my sword)* ought to be; if the great noise is anything to go by, they must be shouting about someone important.

23 **And more I beg not** That's all I ask.

24 **gently rendered** has surrendered peaceably *(or even 'tamely')*

27 **The day almost ...** It is almost possible to declare the victory yours.

28–29 **foes That strike beside us** soldiers in Macbeth's army who either (1) deliberately strike so as to miss us; or (2) fight on our side

Act 5 Scene 7

They fight, and YOUNG SIWARD is slain.

MACBETH   Thou wast born of woman: –
But swords I smile at, weapons laugh to scorn,
Brandished by man that's of a woman born.

Exit.

Alarms. Enter MACDUFF.

MACDUFF   That way the noise is. – (*Calling to* MACBETH) Tyrant,
                show thy face:
            If thou be'st slain, and with no stroke of mine,   15
            My wife and children's ghosts will haunt me still.
            I cannot strike at wretched Kernes, whose arms
            Are hired to bear their staves: either thou, Macbeth,
            Or else my sword, with an unbattered edge,
            I sheathe again undeeded. There thou shouldst be;   20
            By this great clatter, one of greatest note
            Seems bruited. (*Aside*) Let me find him, Fortune!
            And more I beg not.

Exit. Alarm.

Enter MALCOLM and OLD SIWARD.

SIWARD   This way, my lord; – the castle's gently rendered:
            The tyrant's people on both sides do fight;   25
            The noble thanes do bravely in the war.
            The day almost itself professes yours,
            And little is to do.

MALCOLM   We have met with foes
            That strike beside us.

SIWARD   Enter, Sir, the castle.

Exeunt. Alarm.

5.8 Dunsinane – outside the castle

Macbeth finally faces Macduff, who dismays him by revealing that his was a Caesarean birth. Macbeth at first refuses to fight.

Activities

Character review: Macbeth (21)

Discuss what the following lines suggest about Macbeth at this point:

- 1–3: about suicide
- 4–6: that he is feeling a conscience about killing Macduff's family? or that he is actually afraid of Macduff and finding reasons not to fight him?
- 17–22: about his attitude to the Witches
- 27–29: about the choice between captivity and death.

Derek Jacobi as Macbeth in 1993

1–2 play the Roman fool ... *Romans would commit suicide rather than suffer the humiliation of defeat.*

2–3 Whiles I see lives ... While I can see living enemies, the wounds will look better upon them (than upon myself).

8 Thou losest labour You are wasting your efforts.

9–11 As easy may'st thou ... It would be as easy to cut the uncuttable air with your sword as it would be to wound me. Let your blade fall on the helmets of men who can be wounded (**vulnerable crests**).

16 Untimely ripped *Macduff was delivered prematurely, by a Caesarean operation.*

18 For it hath cowed ... subdued my spirit

19 juggling deceiving *(juggling with words)*

20 palter ... in a double sense cheat us with double meanings

21–22 That keep the word ... It sounds as though they are keeping their word, but, when it comes to it, our hopes are dashed.

Scene 8

Another part of the field.

Enter MACBETH.

MACBETH　　Why should I play the Roman fool, and die
　　　　　　On mine own sword? Whiles I see lives, the gashes
　　　　　　Do better upon them.

Enter MACDUFF.

MACDUFF　　　　　　　　　　　　Turn, hell-hound, turn!

MACBETH　　Of all men else I have avoided thee:
　　　　　　But get thee back, my soul is too much charged　　5
　　　　　　With blood of thine already.

MACDUFF　　　　　　　　　　　　I have no words;
　　　　　　My voice is in my sword: thou bloodier villain
　　　　　　Than terms can give thee out!

They fight.

MACBETH　　　　　　　　　　　　Thou losest labour:
　　　　　　As easy may'st thou the intrenchant air
　　　　　　With thy keen sword impress, as make me bleed:　　10
　　　　　　Let fall thy blade on vulnerable crests:
　　　　　　I bear a charmèd life, which must not yield
　　　　　　To one of woman born.

MACDUFF　　　　　　　　　　　　Despair thy charm;
　　　　　　And let the angel whom thou still hast served
　　　　　　Tell thee, Macduff was from his mother's womb　　15
　　　　　　Untimely ripped.

MACBETH　　Accursèd be that tongue that tells me so,
　　　　　　For it hath cowed my better part of man:
　　　　　　And be these juggling fiends no more believed,
　　　　　　That palter with us in a double sense,　　20
　　　　　　That keep the word of promise to our ear,
　　　　　　And break it to our hope. – I'll not fight with thee.

MACDUFF　　Then yield thee, coward,
　　　　　　And live to be the show and gaze o' th' time:
　　　　　　We'll have thee, as our rarer monsters are,　　25

5.9 Dunsinane – within the castle

Rather than submit to Malcolm and be humiliated, Macbeth fights on and is killed. Rosse informs Old Siward that his son is dead.

Activities

Actors' interpretations (33): Macbeth's death

According to Shakespeare's script, Macbeth dies offstage and his head is brought on in the final scene (5.9.19). Many productions, though, decide to show Macbeth dying at Macduff's hands on stage. Piers Ibbotson, Assistant Director of the 1994 RSC production, felt that: 'For Elizabethan audiences the sight of a severed head on stage would have a horrifying effect. For twentieth-century audiences a severed head makes us think of horror movies.'

In the 1994 production, Derek Jacobi's Macbeth embraced death willingly and seemed to commit suicide in a self-inflicted blow on the words 'Hold, enough!' (34).

Discuss whether you think Macbeth's death should take place on stage or off. Consider:

- Piers Ibbotson's comment about severed heads
- the fact that they are rarely realistic
- whether our view of Macbeth or Macduff might be changed (perhaps increasing sympathy for Macbeth) if the killing were to take place on stage
- whether you think it is likely that Macbeth would welcome death, like a kind of suicide.

26 **Painted upon a pole ...** you'll have your picture hung on a pole with writing underneath

29 **baited with the rabble's curse** taunted and cursed by stupid, common people

31–32 **And thou ...** and even if you, who are not born of woman, are fighting me, I will still battle to the end (**try the last**)

33 **lay on** start fighting

34 **"Hold, enough!"** 'Stop! I give in!'

Retreat. Flourish. Trumpets sound the end of the fighting; then there is a fanfare for Malcolm's entrance.

1 **I would ...** I wish our missing friends had returned safely.

2–3 **Some must go off ...** Some have to die; but, judging by the bodies here, we have won a great victory with little loss.

5 **... paid a soldier's debt** He has given what he owed: his life.

7–9 **The which no sooner ...** and no sooner had he confirmed his manhood by his bravery (**prowess**) – sticking unflinchingly to his post – than he died like a man.

10–11 **Your cause of sorrow ...** You must not mourn for him as much as he deserves, or you will never stop mourning.

12 **before** on the front of his body (*proving that he was not running away*)

Painted upon a pole, and underwrit,
"Here may you see the tyrant".

MACBETH   I will not yield,
To kiss the ground before young Malcolm's feet,
And to be baited with the rabble's curse.
Though Birnam wood be come to Dunsinane,   30
And thou opposed, being of no woman born,
Yet I will try the last: before my body
I throw my warlike shield: lay on, Macduff;
And damned be him that first cries, "Hold, enough!"

Exeunt, fighting. Alarms. Re-enter fighting, and MACBETH is slain.

Scene 9

Within the castle.

*Retreat. Flourish. Enter, with drum and colours, MALCOLM, OLD
SIWARD, ROSSE, thanes and soldiers.*

MALCOLM   I would the friends we miss were safe arrived.

SIWARD   Some must go off; and yet, by these I see,
So great a day as this is cheaply bought.

MALCOLM   Macduff is missing, and your noble son.

ROSSE   Your son, my lord, has paid a soldier's debt: 5
He only lived but till he was a man;
The which no sooner had his prowess confirmed,
In the unshrinking station where he fought,
But like a man he died.

SIWARD   Then he is dead?

ROSSE   Ay, and brought off the field. Your cause of sorrow   10
Must not be measured by his worth, for then
It hath no end.

SIWARD   Had he his hurts before?

ROSSE   Ay, on the front.

SIWARD   Why, then, God's soldier be he!

5.9 Dunsinane – within the castle

As Old Siward expresses his pride that his son died bravely, Macduff enters with Macbeth's severed head. Malcolm rewards the loyal thanes by creating them earls, explains what now has to be done, and invites everyone to his coronation.

Activities

Actors' interpretations (34): the ending

Stage the final moment of the play, after Malcolm's speech, to bring out three different interpretations:

- that there will now be peace and harmony in Scotland
- that Malcolm will not be strong enough to prevent civil war from breaking out
- that Malcolm will himself prove to be a tyrant.

Stage any other possible interpretations and discuss which seems to fit best your overall view of the play and its meanings.

---

16 **his knell is knolled** his funeral bell has tolled

21 **usurper** *someone who kills or deposes a rightful king and takes his place*

the time the world

22–24 **I see thee compassed ...** I see you are surrounded by the kingdom's finest nobles (**pearl**). I am speaking their thoughts; and I ask for their voices to join with mine in saying ...

26–27 **We shall not spend ...** I will not waste much time before rewarding you individually for your love, and giving you what I owe you.

31 **Which would be planted newly ...** which ought to be given a new start in this new era

34 **Producing forth ...** bringing out of hiding the cruel agents (**ministers**)

37–38 **what needful else That calls ...** what other necessary matters demand my attention

39 **in measure ...** in the proper order, at the right time and in the right place.

          Had I as many sons as I have hairs,
          I would not wish them to a fairer death: 15
          And so, his knell is knolled.

MALCOLM   He's worth more sorrow,
          And that I'll spend for him.

SIWARD   He's worth no more;
          They say he parted well, and paid his score:
          And so, God be with him! – Here comes newer
             comfort.

Enter MACDUFF with MACBETH's head.

MACDUFF   Hail, King! for so thou art. Behold, where stands   20
          Th' usurper's cursèd head: the time is free.
          I see thee compassed with thy kingdom's pearl,
          That speak my salutation in their minds;
          Whose voices I desire aloud with mine, –
          Hail, King of Scotland!

ALL   Hail, King of Scotland!   25

Flourish.

MALCOLM   We shall not spend a large expense of time
          Before we reckon with your several loves,
          And make us even with you. My thanes and kinsmen,
          Henceforth be earls, the first that ever Scotland
          In such an honour named. What's more to do,   30
          Which would be planted newly with the time, –
          As calling home our exiled friends abroad,
          That fled the snares of watchful tyranny;
          Producing forth the cruel ministers
          Of this dead butcher, and his fiend-like queen,   35
          Who, as 't is thought, by self and violent hands
          Took off her life; – this, and what needful else
          That calls upon us, by the grace of Grace,
          We will perform in measure, time and place,
          So thanks to all at once, and to each one,   40
          Whom we invite to see us crowned at Scone.

Flourish. Exeunt.

Exam practice

Character review: Malcolm (4)

A Discuss what part Malcolm has played in the downfall of Macbeth and what now has to be done, according to his speech (5.9.26–41), to restore the country to health.

B Imagine you are Malcolm. Write down in your own words the notes that you make in preparation for your first speech to the Scottish thanes (the one delivered in lines 26–41 of 5.9), in which you jot down ideas about:
- the need to reward people who have supported you (see 26–30)
- plans to recall people in exile and other friends (30–33)
- punishing the guilty (34–35)
- revealing more details about Macbeth and Lady Macbeth (36–37)
- planning the coronation and dealing with other issues (37–41).

For each of the above items, add details known from the plot, and include opinions which Malcolm would be likely to voice.

C From what you have learned of Malcolm, how far do you see him as an ideal ruler? Assess his strengths and discuss whether he has any significant weaknesses in an essay which also considers how optimistic an audience can be about his future rule.

Character review: Lady Macbeth (11)

At 5.5.7 there is a cry of women and Seyton reports 'The queen, my lord, is dead.' (16). Shakespeare's script does not tell us the manner of her death (although Malcolm later reports – 5.9.36–37 – that she is said to have committed suicide), but there have been many theories put forward.

Brid Brennan as Lady Macbeth in 1996

(A) Discuss how you think she might have died and how her death might be represented in a film version of *Macbeth*.

(B) Write a final letter from Lady Macbeth to her husband.

(C) Imagine that Shakespeare had written a death scene for Lady Macbeth. Discuss (a) what it might have consisted of; (b) what she would have said in her dying speech; and (c) why you think Shakespeare did not include such a death scene.

Shakespeare's language: imagery (2)

5.2 continues the imagery to do with clothing, disease, and natural growth, to be found throughout the play.

(A) Draw a cartoon to bring out the meaning of one of the following and discuss why the image is effective in conveying the particular idea:

*   now does he feel his title
  Hang loose about him, like a giant's robe
  Upon a dwarfish thief. (20–22)

* Meet we the medicine of the sickly weal;
  And with him pour we, in our country's purge,
  Each drop of us. (27–29)

*   Or so much as it needs
  To dew the sovereign flower and drown the weeds. (29–30)

(B) Draw two cartoons. The first is to bring out the meaning of the clothing image from 1.7:

*   and I have bought
  Golden opinions from all sorts of people,
  Which would be worn now in their newest gloss,
  Not cast aside so soon. (32–35)

The second is based on the image in 5.2:

* He cannot buckle his distempered cause
  Within the belt of rule. (15–16)

Discuss the differences between the two pictures and what they show about the changes that have overtaken Macbeth.

(C) Discuss the links between the imagery of clothing, disease, and natural growth, and the themes of (a) disorder; and (b) kingship.

Plot review (7)

Complete a graph which plots (a) how powerful; and (b) how happy and contented, Macbeth is as the play develops. Grade the y-axis from 0 to 10 (10 being most powerful and happiest), and mark important points in the story along the x-axis (such as 1.2.70; the end of 1.3; etc.). Plot different coloured lines for power and happiness and compare your version with other people's.

Activities

Thinking about the play as a whole . . .

Actors' interpretations

1 **Ⓐ** *Staging a scene*

Pick your favourite scene from the play and draw a sketch to show what a key moment might look like, adding notes to explain details of the characters' actions, expressions and gestures.

Ⓑ *Staging for contrast*

Pick two contrasting moments from the play (perhaps one near the beginning and one near the end) and, using the outline or plan on page 198, show how the moments might be staged to bring out the contrasts, writing annotations to explain your decisions.

Ⓒ *Directing an extract*

Annotate a short scene or extract to show actors' movements, actions and reactions. Introduce it with a statement about the particular interpretation that you are aiming for (such as a pessimistic ending to the play).

2 **Ⓐ** *Casting the play*

If you had the chance to direct a performance of *Macbeth* on stage, which actors and actresses would you cast in the various roles? Make decisions about each character, explaining why you think the particular performer would be right for the part.

Ⓑ *A theatre programme*

Create a theatre programme for a production of *Macbeth*. This might include:

- a cast list with the names of the actors
- some background material (for example, on witches and witchcraft in Shakespeare's time – see page 200; or articles on the wordplay or some of the major themes)
- details about Shakespeare and his plays (see page 211).

ⓒ *A newspaper review*

Write a review of *Macbeth*, as a response to an actual theatre performance, or any one of the video versions that you have seen.

3 Filming the play

There have been many different film adaptations of the *Macbeth* story: *Throne of Blood* (1957) was a Japanese film set in the period of samurai warriors; in *Joe Macbeth* (1956), the story was translated to the Chicago gangster world; and in *Umabatha* (1972) Shakespeare's characters became Zulus.

Plan a modern film adaptation of *Macbeth* (possibly on the lines of Baz Luhrmann's *Romeo and Juliet*), thinking about an appropriate setting.

(a) Make decisions about actors to play the roles and locations for the different scenes of the story.

(b) Storyboard one of the key sequences and bring out the special qualities of your new interpretation.

(c) Discuss which features of the play (not only the story, but its themes and language) you would hope to bring out most successfully and which would be harder to get across.

4 **Ⓐ** *An advertisement*

Create a magazine advert for a new production of *Macbeth*, featuring some of your favourite actors. First look at some examples in magazines, to see how images are used and what written material is included.

Ⓑ *Video covers*

Discuss the two covers of video versions of *Macbeth* on page 180.

- Which features of the story do they seem to be concentrating on?
- Which characters have they decided to highlight?
- How have they arranged the images?
- What text have they used to 'sell' the product?

Create a video cover for your own screen production of the play (which might feature some of the performers chosen for activity A).

Activities

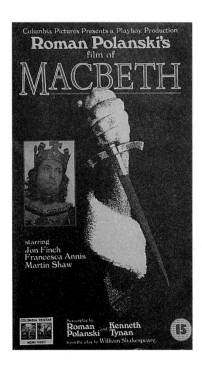

C *A display*

Put together a classroom display on *Macbeth*, which would be interesting for a younger class approaching the play for the first time. Include:

- any drawings that you have done (stage designs, storyboards . . .)
- other background work (Macbeth's first letter to his wife; reports of the battle; newspaper articles from the time; diary entries . . .)
- anything else you can think of (a poster advertising the play; cartoons of images . . .)
- things that you have collected from productions (production postcards, programmes, reviews . . .).

You will need to write some introductory material, explaining what the play is about and how the various elements of the display tie in.

Character reviews

5 Character profiles

Some actors write systematic notes about the characters they are preparing to play. Draw up a Character Profile form on a word-processor and then fill it in for any characters you are working on. Headings might be:

NAME:
SOCIAL POSITION:
SUPER-OBJECTIVE: (the character's overriding aim, which drives them on: e.g. 'to become king')
LINE OF ACTION: (the practical things they must do to achieve that aim: e.g. 'kill Duncan . . .')
OBSTACLES AGAINST IT: (e.g. 'He is a good king...')
WHAT THE CHARACTER SAYS ABOUT HERSELF/HIMSELF:
WHAT OTHER CHARACTERS SAY ABOUT HER/HIM:
IMPRESSION ON FIRST APPEARANCE:
RELATIONSHIPS WITH OTHERS:
OTHER INFORMATION:

6 Character review: Macbeth

Ⓐ A short biography

Make a list of Macbeth's virtues and strengths – as they are described in 1.2 and 1.4 – and compare them with a list of his crimes and weaknesses, from 1.5 onwards. Then write a short biography of him for an encyclopedia.

Ⓑ Two obituaries

Draft two obituaries on Macbeth: one from a pro-Malcolm newspaper; one from another newspaper (perhaps in a foreign country) which admired Macbeth. Think about the different ways in which each one would select facts about his rule and the ways in which those facts would be presented.

Ⓒ A complex figure

What does Malcolm's description of Macbeth as 'this dead butcher' (5.9.35) leave out? Write a study of Macbeth which illustrates why he is so interesting and complex a figure.

Activities

7 Character review: Macbeth

Macbeth says 'I have supped full with horrors' (5.5.13). Look back through the play to recap on the horrors that Macbeth has seen and been responsible for, and then create a display, for which this quotation is the title. Include in it:

- extracts from Macbeth's secret diaries (in which he records events about which no other character can know)
- reports by his enemies on what is happening in Scotland
- the doctor's reports on Lady Macbeth
- extracts from other characters' letters
- anything else which you think will add to the representation of the horrors in *Macbeth.*

8 Character review: Lady Macbeth

C *Time line*

Look back at each of Lady Macbeth's appearances in the play and make notes on the ways in which she moves from being apparently very strong and in control to being very sick and troubled, noting also the main events which seem to affect her. Then draw up a time line of the play which records 'The decline of Lady Macbeth'.

B *The gentlewoman's record*

Imagine you are Lady Macbeth's gentlewoman (who talks with the doctor in 5.1). Write your own record of what happened to your mistress, from the moment when Macbeth wrote to inform her that Duncan would be staying under their roof. Decide first how far you might find yourself on Lady Macbeth's side.

C *Loneliness and sympathy*

Sinéad Cusack felt that the end of Lady Macbeth's story was: 'Lonely, so lonely ... utter desolation.' Discuss the part that loneliness plays in her decline and weigh it against the other factors in a piece of writing which also addresses the question of whether you feel any sympathy for her.

9 Character review: Macbeth and Lady Macbeth

A *Their relationship*

Look back at the scenes in which Macbeth and Lady Macbeth appear together and jot down one or two statements per scene which reveal something about their relationship at that point in the play.

B *Changes in their relationship*

Write a piece of dialogue between the porter and Lady Macbeth's gentlewoman (who appears in 5.1) in which they discuss the changes that they have noticed in the Macbeths' relationship since just after the battle against the rebels. Decide first what they would know about and what they might be able to guess at.

C *Explaining the changes*

Write an account of the ways in which the relationship between Macbeth and Lady Macbeth changes from the beginning to the end of the play and try to explain these changes.

10 Character review: the witches

Before tackling these activities, read the section about Witches and witchcraft on page 200.

A *Powers*

Look back at the scenes in which the Witches appear and make a list of the powers they seem to possess. Find examples of where, in the course of the play, they are possibly using the power to:

- encourage people to deal with evil spirits
- stop them praying
- make them see visions
- make them physically stressed
- take away their will to live.

B *Reactions of a Witch*

Imagine you are one of the Witches. Write your thoughts at three moments in the play: the beginning, as you plan to meet Macbeth (1.1 and 1.3); after you have uttered your prophecies and have left him (1.3.78); and after you have shown him the apparitions (4.1.132). Then write the outline of a scene to take place after Macbeth's death and Malcolm's first speech as King (a new 5.10), in which we see your reactions to events.

C *The Witches' role and witchcraft in society*

The director Tyrone Guthrie removed the first Witches' scene, believing that, to open the play with the Witches, was to acknowledge them as 'a governing influence of the tragedy'. Write a study of the part they do play, assessing how far they are, in your opinion, responsible for what happens and how far merely predicting what *will* happen.

11 Character review: the porter

Why should Shakespeare have included the porter scene? What effect
does it have? Discuss each of these possible reasons and grade them on a
scale of 1 (very unlikely) to 5 (very likely):

Practical factors for including the scene

(a) It gives the actors playing Macbeth and Lady Macbeth time to get off
stage, wash the blood off and change their clothes.
(b) Shakespeare had comic actors in his company; they were popular with
audiences and it was sensible to give them a part in each play.
(c) King James would be pleased by the references to the Gunpowder
Plot.

Dramatic reasons

(d) By letting the audience laugh after the horror of seeing the blood-
spattered Macbeths, they will be more able to accept further bloodshed
and horror in the scenes which follow.
(e) The humour is used as a 'laughter-conductor' to prevent the audience
from giggling in the wrong place (especially later in the scene).
(f) The porter's speeches reflect in comic form some of the key ideas in
the play, such as damnation, equivocation and the supernatural.
(g) By making him the porter of hell-gate, a link is made between
Macbeth's castle and hell – remember, Lady Macbeth has called upon
'murdering ministers' (1.5.47).
(h) The porter would remind Shakespeare's audience of the traditional
figure of the porter of hell-gate in medieval plays and this would make
the story universal: it is about all of us, not just Macbeth and his wife.
(i) The topical references to the Gunpowder Plot and equivocators would
remind the audience about the horror of attempting to kill a king.
(j) The reference to treason links with the earlier account of the Thane of
Cawdor and a later discussion between Lady Macduff and her son (4.2).
(k) The farmer links with the theme of nature and the tailor with the
clothing imagery.
(l) Drink 'provokes the desire, but it takes away the performance'; the
contrast between desire and act is frequently made in the play, and is
typical of the frequent use of antithesis.

Use these points to write an essay on the contribution that the porter's
scene can make to a production of *Macbeth*.

12 Character review: Duncan, Banquo, Malcolm, Macduff and Rosse

Ⓐ *Good qualities and weaknesses*

These are usually portrayed as 'good' characters, contrasted with Macbeth's evil. Look back through the scenes in which they appear and list each person's good qualities. Then discuss which weaknesses each one might be said to display.

Ⓑ *Acting opportunities, a dossier and obituaries*

(a) What opportunities are there for actors playing these characters? Pick one, look at the scenes in which he appears and describe what satisfaction or enjoyment exists in playing the part. (You could write this from the actor's point of view, using his 'voice'.)

(b) After he comes to power, Macbeth has a paid spy in the household of anyone he mistrusts – perhaps all the other thanes. Create the dossier that such a spy might write on any one of these characters (except Duncan).

(c) Write two versions of Duncan's obituary – first from a newspaper loyal to him, then from one controlled by Macbeth.

Ⓒ *Make a character 'bad'*

Construct an argument for making one of these characters ambiguous or openly 'bad'. Cite evidence from the script which would make such an interpretation possible and consider what might be gained and lost by such an approach in terms of the overall interpretation of the play.

Shakespeare's language

13 Features

Ⓐ *A poster*

Look back through the play and find an example of each of the following:

- antithesis (look at the activities on page 10)
- imagery (see pages 4, 177)
- dramatic irony (see page 18)
- euphemism (see page 30)
- ambiguity (see page 39)
- irony (see page 102)

Activities

Create a poster for the classroom with the title 'Shakespeare's language in
Macbeth', which includes the three examples, with a brief written account
and a drawing which explains how each one works and how it helps to get
the meaning across.

Ⓑ *Imagery*

Look back at the activities to do with imagery (pages 4 and 177) and write
an essay explaining how the images in the play help to convey its
meanings.

Ⓒ *A reference work, antithesis and imagery*

Collect together the written material that you have compiled:

* examples of antithesis, ambiguity and euphemism
* examples of dramatic irony
* work on imagery
* any other notes or background materials.

(a) Using a word-processor, compile a reference work on 'Shakespeare's
   language in *Macbeth*' which would be useful to anybody studying the
   play at Key Stage 3.

(b) Write an essay on one of the following: either the importance of
   antithesis in providing an underlying sense of disorder; or the range of
   imagery in the play and ways in which it affects our understanding of
   characters and themes.

14 Verse and prose

(a) Read the section on page 203 and look back through the play at all the
   moments where Shakespeare uses prose rather than verse. Consider
   what effect this use of prose has, looking particularly at:

   * what differences there are between the various prose sections in
     terms of the style of speech (e.g. compare the porter with Lady
     Macduff)
   * why it seems appropriate to use prose in each case, rather than verse
   * what effects are achieved by switching from verse to prose (e.g. look
     at the end of 2.2 and the beginning of 2.3)
   * whether there are any 'rules' for the use of prose.

(b) Read the section on verse on pages 201–203. Then list the main
   characteristics of the Witches' verse. Think about:

   * rhyme
   * metre (the number of 'beats' in the line)
   * unusual vocabulary

- use of antithesis
- any other features you can think of.

Write an account of the Witches' verse, discussing these characteristics and showing how the verse helps to convey a feeling of the supernatural and the sense of inexorable (unavoidable) fate.

(c) Re-read the activities on pages 32, 42, 74 and 162 and write a study of the soliloquies showing how they are used to reflect Macbeth's changing state of mind.

Themes

15 A theme is an important subject which seems to arise at several times in the play, showing in what the characters do and the language they use, so that we receive different perspectives on it. Themes in *Macbeth* include the following:

- Appearance and reality (1.5 etc.)
- Equivocation (2.3 etc.)
- Nature (2.4 etc.)
- Order (3.4; 4.1 etc.)
- Kingship (4.3 etc.).

There are also *key words* to be found throughout the play, which help to reveal some of the obsessions and preoccupations of the characters. In Macbeth these include: 'blood', 'sleep', 'man' and many references to animals.

A *A theme collage*

Draw up a spider diagram which includes all the many references you can find to any one theme in the play. Then create a collage which illustrates how the theme is developed and explored.

B *Analysing a theme*

Select one theme and write about:

- how it is developed and explored in the play
- what it adds to your overall interpretation of the play's meanings.

Activities

c *Themes and key words*

Write an account of the themes and key words in *Macbeth*, showing how
the themes are developed and the key words recur, to contribute to the
overall meanings of the play.

Plot review

16 **A** *Newspaper headlines*

Imagine that there had been tabloid newspapers in Macbeth's day. Write a
series of headlines that might have appeared, starting with the day after
the battle against the rebels in Act 1 and ending with Malcolm's
announcement about the coronation at the end of the play. Make sure you
include headlines on dramatic background events such as the strange
happenings the night of Duncan's murder.

B *Radio reports*

Write a series of brief radio reports which might have been broadcast over
the World Service in Macbeth's time. Each one should be no more than
two or three sentences long, but should summarise the most important
news of the day. If possible, record your reports and include brief
interviews where appropriate.

C *Television programme*

How might a serious television current affairs programme in England have
handled some of the events portrayed in *Macbeth*? Pick an appropriate
moment (such as the day after Macbeth's coronation, or the moment when
Macduff arrives in King Edward's court) and draft the script for a
programme which includes factual reports from a correspondent in
Scotland and interviews with appropriate people. Finally perform the script.

17 *Macbeth* does not have a sub-plot and the main events are fairly easy to
recall. Re-tell the story as:

A *Acrostic*

Compile a 'MACBETH' acrostic – in this case, a seven-line poem, the first
line beginning with M, then A, then C . . . and so on.

B *Mini-saga*

Write a mini-saga – a prose story of *exactly* fifty words, no more, no less.

C *Sonnet*

Compose a sonnet similar to the one at the beginning of *Romeo and Juliet*.

18 Shakespeare seems to have got his main story from a popular historian called Raphael Holinshed. These are some of the main 'facts' that Shakespeare would have gained from Holinshed's account (which is not historically accurate). Discuss the changes that Shakespeare made when he came to write his play, and the effects that these changes had.

Points from Holinshed's *Chronicles of England, Scotland and Ireland*:

- Duncan was a young man and a fairly weak and ineffectual ruler.
- There are three main battles during Duncan's reign: the defeat of Macdonwald's rebellion; the defeat of the Norwegian invaders; and the defeat of the Danes.
- Macbeth has a justifiable claim to the throne through his wife (granddaughter of a previous king) and her son by her first husband.
- There was no system of 'primogeniture' (in which the eldest son always inherits the throne) in Macbeth's day.
- Banquo and others were accomplices in Duncan's murder, which was regarded as a political assassination.
- Macbeth ruled as a successful and good king for ten years. (He actually reigned for seventeen years: 1040–57.)
- Macduff refused to assist in the building of Dunsinane Castle and so Macbeth surrounded Macduff's castle with a great army.
- The testing of Malcolm occurs after Macduff has been told of his wife's death.
- Macbeth is killed by Macduff after fleeing from Dunsinane.

There is no account in Holinshed of Banquo's ghost returning, nor Lady Macbeth's sleepwalking and death; and the death of Duncan is taken from a totally different killing: Donwald's murder of King Duff.

Background to Shakespeare

Do some research in an encyclopedia or CD-ROM to find out more about the background features highlighted in **bold**.
There are also activities for additional research.

Shakespeare's England

Shakespeare lived during a period called the **Renaissance**: a time when extraordinary changes were taking place, especially in the fields of religion, politics, science, language and the arts. He wrote during the reigns of **Elizabeth I** and **James I**.

Religion and politics

- In the century following the **Reformation** and England's break with Rome in the 1530s, people in Shakespeare's England began to view the world and their own place in it very differently.

- Queen Elizabeth restored the **Protestant religion** in England, begun under her father Henry VIII.

- England had become a proud and independent nation, and a leading military and trading power, especially after the defeat of the **Spanish Armada** in 1588.

- There were divisions in the Protestant Church, with extremist groups such as the **Puritans** disapproving of much of what they saw in society and the Church.

- James I succeeded Elizabeth in 1603. He was a Scot, interested in witchcraft, and a supporter of the theatre, who fought off the treasonous attempt of the **Gunpowder Plot** in 1605.

- People began to question traditional beliefs about rank and social order – ideas that some people should be considered superior simply because they were born into wealthy families; or that those in power should always be obeyed without question.

- As trade became increasingly important, it was not only the nobility who could become wealthy. People could move around the country more easily and a competitive **capitalist economy** developed.

Science and discovery

- Scientists began to question traditional authorities (the accepted ideas handed down from one generation to the next) and depended instead upon their own observation of the world, especially after the development of instruments such as the telescope. **Galileo** came into conflict with the Church for claiming that the Earth was not the centre of the universe.
- Explorers and traders brought back new produce, such as spices and silks, and created great excitement in the popular imagination for stories of distant lands and their peoples.

Language

- The more traditional scholars still regarded **Latin** as the only adequate language for scholarly discussion and writing (and liked it because it also prevented many 'uncultured' people from understanding philosophy, medicine, etc.).
- A new interest in the **English language** came with England's growing importance and sense of identity.
- The Protestants favoured a personal relationship with God, which meant being able to read the Bible themselves (rather than letting priests interpret it for them). This led to the need for a good version in English, and **The Authorised Version of the Bible** (the 'King James Bible') was published in 1611.
- **Grammar schools** sprang up after the Reformation which increased literacy (but mostly among males in the middle and upper classes, and mainly in London).
- The invention of the **printing press** in the 1450s had led to more people having access to information and new ideas – not just the scholars.
- The English language began to be standardised in this period (into **Standard English**), but it was still very flexible and there was less insistence on following rules than there is nowadays.

- There was an enormous expansion in **vocabulary**, which affected every area of daily life: crafts, sciences, technology, trade, philosophy, food ...
- English vocabulary was enriched by numerous **borrowings** from other languages. Between 1500 and 1650, over 10,000 new words entered the language (though many later fell out of use). Some 'purists' (who disliked change) opposed the introduction of new words.

Use a dictionary to find where the words for common foods came from: coffee, tea, tomato, chocolate, potato ...

- Shakespeare therefore lived through a time when the English vocabulary was expanding amazingly and the grammar was still flexible, a time when people were intensely excited by language.

Shakespeare's plays reflect this fascination for words. Do some research to find examples of: Mercutio's wit in *Romea and Juliet*; Dogberry's slip-ups in *Much Ado About Nothing*; Shylock's fatal bond and Portia's 'escape clause' in *The Merchant of Venice*; the puzzling oracle in *The Winter's Tale*; and Bottom's problems with words ('I see a voice!') in *A Midsummer Night's Dream*.

Plays and playhouses

The theatre was a very popular form of entertainment in Shakespeare's time, with audiences drawn from all classes of people. The theatre buildings and the companies of actors were different from what we are used to today.

The theatres

- The professional theatre was based exclusively in London, which had around 200,000 inhabitants in 1600.
- It was often under attack from the **Puritan**-dominated Guildhall, which wanted to abolish the theatres totally because, in their opinion, they encouraged sinful behaviour.

- Acting companies first performed in the courtyards of coaching inns, in the halls of great houses, in churches, at markets and in the streets. The first outdoor playhouse was The Red Lion, built in c.1567 (when Shakespeare was three).
- By 1600, there were eleven public outdoor theatres, including **the Rose**, the Swan and the Globe (Shakespeare's theatre).
- **Shakespeare's Globe** opened in 1599 on Maiden Lane, Bankside, and was destroyed by fire during a performance of *Henry VIII* in 1613. (No one was killed, but a bottle of ale was needed to put out a fire in a man's breeches!). See pages 195–198.
- Some outdoor theatres held audiences of up to 3,000.
- Standing room was one penny; the gallery twopence; the 'Lords' Room' threepence; and it was more expensive still to sit on the stage. This was at a time when a joiner (skilled carpenter) might earn 6s to 8s (72 to 96 pence) per week. By 1614, it was 6d ($2^1/_2$ pence) for the newly opened indoor Hope Theatre.

Work out whether it was cheaper or more expensive to go to the theatre in Shakespeare's time than it is today. (To do the comparison, you will need to find out (a) how much the cheapest and most expensive tickets are at the Royal Shakespeare Theatre, Stratford-upon-Avon, for example; and (b) what a skilled worker might earn nowadays.)

- Outdoor theatre performances usually started about 2 pm or 3 pm (there was no artificial light).
- The season started in September, through to the beginning of Lent; then from after Easter to early summer. (Theatres were closed during outbreaks of **the plague**: 11,000 died of the plague in summer 1593 and the theatres remained almost completely closed until 1594.) Some companies went on summer tours, playing in inns, etc.
- The majority of theatres were closed during the **Civil War**, in 1642 (and most of the playhouses were demolished by 1656).
- There were some indoor theatres (called 'private' or 'hall' theatres) such as the **Blackfriars**, which was used up to 1609 almost exclusively by child actors (the minimum entrance fee of sixpence indicates a wealthier audience). Plays developed which were more suited to the more intimate atmosphere, with the stage illuminated by artificial lighting.
- The star actor **Richard Burbage** and his brother Cuthbert had the licence of the Blackfriars from 1596 and Shakespeare's later plays were performed there.

Work out from pages 211–212 which of Shakespeare's plays might have been written with the indoor Blackfriars theatre in mind.

The actors

- In 1572 parliament passed an Act 'For the Punishment of Vagabonds'. As actors were classed as little better than wandering beggars, this Act required them to be attached to a theatre company and have the patronage (financial support and protection) of someone powerful. This meant that companies had to keep on the right side of patrons and make sure they didn't offend the Master of the Revels, who was responsible for **censorship**.

- Major companies in Shakespeare's time included the Admiral's Men and the Queen's Men. **The Lord Chamberlain's Men** (the group that Shakespeare joined, later known as **the King's Men** when James came to the throne) was formed in 1594 and was run by shareholders (called 'the housekeepers').

- The Burbages held 50 per cent of the shares of the company; the remaining 50 per cent was divided mainly between the actors, including Shakespeare himself, who owned about 10 per cent – which helped to earn him a comfortable regular income.

Acting

- There was very little rehearsal time, with several plays 'in repertory' (being performed) in any given period.

- We don't actually know about the style of acting, but modern, naturalistic, low-key acting was not possible on the Globe stage. At the same time, Shakespeare appears to be mocking over-the-top delivery in at least two of his plays.

Read *Hamlet* 3.2 (Hamlet's first three speeches to the First Player) and *A Midsummer Night's Dream* (especially Act 5).

- Actors certainly needed to be aware of their relationship with the audience: there must have been plenty of direct contact. In a daylight theatre there can be no pretence that the audience is not there.

Publishing

- Plays were not really regarded as 'literature' in Shakespeare's lifetime, and so the playwright would not have been interested in publishing his plays in book form.
- Some of Shakespeare's plays were, however, originally printed in cheap 'quarto' (pocket-sized) editions. Some were sold officially (under an agreement made between the theatre company and the author), and some pirated (frequently by the actors themselves who had learned most of the script by heart).
- In 1623, seven years after Shakespeare's death, two of his close friends, John Heminges and Henry Condell, collected together the most reliable versions of the plays and published them in a larger size volume known as **the First Folio**. This included eighteen plays which had never before appeared in print, and eighteen more which had appeared in quarto editions. Only *Pericles* was omitted from the plays which make up what we nowadays call Shakespeare's 'Complete Works' (unless we count plays such as *Two Noble Kinsmen*, for which Shakespeare is known to have written some scenes).

Much of the information in these sections comes from Michael Mangan, *A Preface to Shakespeare's Comedies: 1594–1603* Longman, 1996.

The Globe theatre

No one knows precisely what Shakespeare's Globe theatre looked like, but we do have a number of clues:

- a section of the foundations has been unearthed and provides an idea of the size and shape of the outside walls
- the foundations of the Rose, a theatre near the Globe, were excavated in 1988–89

Background to Shakespeare

- a Dutch visitor to Shakespeare's London, called Johannes de Witt, saw a play in the Swan Theatre and made a sketch of the interior.

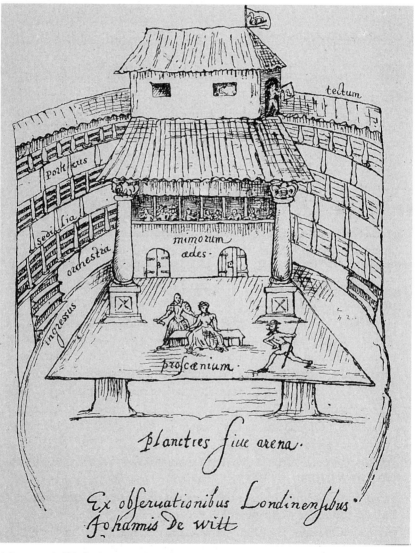

Johannes de Witt's drawing of the Swan

A *The facts*

Using much of the evidence available, a reconstruction of Shakespeare's Globe theatre has been built in London, not far from the site of the original building.

From what you can learn from these photographs:

- Roughly what shape is the theatre, looked at from above?
- How many storeys does it have?
- In which areas can the audience (a) stand, and (b) sit?
- What is behind the stage?
- How much scenery and lighting are used?
- What other details can you pick out which seem to make the Globe different from an indoor theatre (which has a stage at one end, similar to many school assembly halls)?
- Find a copy of Shakespeare's *Henry V* and read the opening speech (by the Chorus) to see what phrase Shakespeare himself famously used to describe the shape of an earlier theatre, the Curtain.

B *Using the stage*

Copy the plan on page 198. Then, using the staging guidelines provided, sketch or mark characters as they might appear at crucial moments in *Macbeth* (such as 2.3.101 or 3.4.49).

C *The actor–audience relationship*

- In what ways is the design of Shakespeare's Globe ideally suited to the performance of his plays?
- How might the open stage and the balcony be useful? (Refer to moments in *Macbeth* or other Shakespeare plays that you know.)
- What do you think would be the most interesting features of the way in which Shakespeare's actors – and those in the reconstructed Globe today – might relate to and interact with the audience? (Which moments in *Macbeth* seem to require a performance in which the audience is very close to the actors, for example?)

Background to Shakespeare

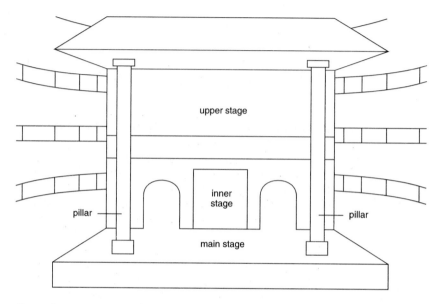

Above: front on view of the stage, as seen by the audience.

Below: bird's-eye view of the stage for positioning of characters.

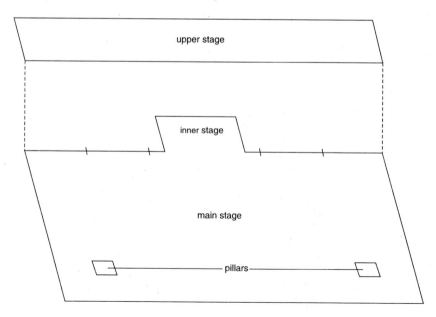

The social and historical background

King James, the Gunpowder Plot and Father Garnet

- King James VI of Scotland succeeded Queen Elizabeth I as James I of England in 1603, the country's first Stuart king.
- In 1605 a group of Catholics, discontented with laws which prevented them from worshipping openly, hid thirty-six barrels of gunpowder in the vaults beneath the House of Lords with the intention of killing the King when he opened Parliament and ultimately seizing power with the aid of Spain. The plot was discovered and the conspirators hunted down and executed, as were many who were thought to have been involved in the plot.
- Notable among these was a Father Garnet who became notorious in his trial for claiming that it had been acceptable to deny his involvement so long as his accusers had had no proof of his guilt, that 'equivocation' of this kind was right and proper if used for a good object, and that, if the law was unjust, a man should not be tried for treason. Garnet was executed in May 1606 and was a major topic of conversation throughout the spring and summer of that year.
- James had a great interest in the theatre and quickly became the new patron of Shakespeare's company, who changed their name accordingly from the Lord Chamberlain's Men to the King's Men. There is some evidence that the first performance of *Macbeth* was at Hampton Court in August 1606 before an audience which included King James and King Christian of Denmark.
- If this is so, it would account for the fact that Shakespeare seems to have included a number of subjects which were known to be of interest to James:
  1. Most obviously, *Macbeth* is a story about the history of Scotland and the origin (in 4.1) of the Stewart dynasty, starting with (the totally mythical) Banquo and coming down to James himself, the eighth Stewart king, with his descendants stretching out in a line apparently forever (The spelling Stuart was adopted by Mary Queen of Scots, King James's mother.) In a court performance, the 'glass' carried by the eighth king might well have been held in front of James so that he could see himself reflected; while the 'two-fold balls and treble sceptres' seem to refer to the double coronation of James in Scotland and England, and the two sceptres used in the English ceremony and the one in the Scottish.

2. James, like all kings, had a personal stake in opposing regicide (the murder of a king) and would no doubt have approved of Macbeth's ultimate downfall and the reminders of the Gunpowder Plot.
3. Malcolm's creation of Scotland's first earls (5.9.29–30) paralleled James's own generosity in giving out honours and titles.
4. James was fascinated by witchcraft.

Witches and witchcraft

- It is important to understand just how seriously people viewed witchcraft in Shakespeare's lifetime and how fascinating the subject was to scholars and to people who considered themselves up-to-date thinkers, such as King James himself.
- In Elizabeth's England, thousands of people (nearly all women) were executed as witches.
- In 1590, while James was still King of Scotland, there were more than 300 witches tortured in order to extract confessions that they were conspiring against the King.
- James took an active part in the trials himself, believing that, since the king was God's representative on earth, he would obviously be the main target of the agents of the devil.
- A year after James came to power, 1604, new laws were enacted stating that practising witches should be executed.
- Many people felt that, if the rule of a king over his people was comparable to God's rule over earth, the man's rule over the family and the head's rule over the body (the mind over the emotions), then witchcraft tried to turn all this upside down, so that the devil rules the earth, women rule the family, and the emotions rule the head.
- James himself wrote and published a book about witchcraft in 1597, the *Demonologie*, in which he detailed their supposed powers of predicting the future, defying normal physical rules, affecting the weather, cursing their enemies and taking demonic possession of otherwise innocent people, all assisted by their 'familiars' (familiar spirits) in the shapes of animals.
- It is not difficult to see that these beliefs appealed to people who were misogynists (women-haters) or who had their own personal interests at heart and used witches as a convenient scapegoat.

Shakespeare's verse

Metre

Every word we use in English can be described according to where the heavy stress falls. For example, these three words (from 1.1–2) have their heavy stress on the first syllable: **capt**ains, **thun**der, **Ban**quo; while in these the heavy stress is on the second syllable: Mac**beth**, ag**ain**, en**ough**.

All Shakespeare's verse has a pattern of light and heavy stresses running through it, known as the metre. You can hear the metre if you read these lines out loud, over-emphasising the heavily stressed syllables:

- So **well** thy **words** be**come** thee, **as** thy **wounds** (1.2.44)
- No **more** that **Thane** of **Caw**dor **shall** de**ceive** (1.2.66)
- And **say** which **grain** will **grow**, and **which** will **not** (1.3.59)

No actor would ever perform the lines in that monotonous way, but they would certainly be aware that the metre was always there, helping to give the verse form and structure.

Sometimes, to point out that a syllable which does not carry a heavy stress in modern English is stressed in Shakespeare's line of verse, it will be accented, like this:

- With twenty trenchèd gashes on his head (3.4.27).

(a) Mark the heavy stresses in that line of the first Murderer's (3.4.27).
(b) The four lines above are all totally regular in their metre: what do you notice about: the pattern of short and heavy stresses? the number of syllables?

Varying the metre

Most of the lines in Shakespeare's plays are not as regular as the four quoted above. In fact, most will have an irregular stress pattern, like this one, where the irregularity perhaps helps the actor to convey the sense of the repeated strokes:

- **Doub**ly re**doub**led **strokes** u**pon** the **foe** (1.2.39).

Occasionally a line will contain an extra syllable (11 rather than 10):

- Till **he** un**seamed** him from the **nave** to the **chaps** (1.2.22)

Here the actor can either try to deliver 'the chaps' as though it were one syllable – th'chaps – (making it a regular line), or emphasise the slowness of the phrase, perhaps underlining its importance.

Some lines stand out, because they are clearly short:

- I cannot tell – (1.2.42)
- What a haste looks through his eyes! (1.2.47)
- It is a peerless kinsman (1.4.58)

A collection of heavy stresses together can add emphasis:

- As **two spent swim**mers, that do **cling to**get**h**er (1.2.8)

Dividing the line into feet

Just as music has a number of beats in a bar, so Shakespeare's verse has five 'feet' in a complete line. A five-foot line is called a 'pentameter' (pent = five; meter = measure).

A single foot can contain syllables from different words, and any one word can be broken up by the foot divisions:

- Dis**dain** | ing **For-** | tune, **with** | his **bran-** | dished **steel** (1.2.17)

This is why a single line of verse is sometimes set out rather oddly in different lines of print, if it is shared between two or more characters, as happens in 2.2:

LADY MACBETH
I heard the owl scream, and the crickets cry.
Did not you speak?

MACBETH   When?
LADY MACBETH   Now.
MACBETH   As I descended?

} line 15

} four
  speeches
  make up
  line 16

Iambic pentameter

A foot which contains an unstressed syllable followed by a stressed one (the standard 'beat': dee-**dum**) is called an 'iamb'. Verse which has five iambs per line as its standard rhythm is called an 'iambic pentameter'.

Iambic pentameter which does not rhyme is also sometimes known as 'blank verse'.

(a) Bearing in mind that the iambic pentameter line goes: dee-**dum**, dee-**dum**, dee-**dum**, dee-**dum**, dee-**dum**, make up some of your own 'Shakespearean' verse (perhaps based on one of the themes of the play).
(b) Copy out the following lines from 1.7 and divide them into five feet; then mark the heavy stresses: lines 6, 15, 20, 21 and – very difficult – line 1.
(c) How many feet are there in the verse spoken by the Witches?

Rhyme

The Witches speak in rhymed verse most of the time and this, combined with the different metre, helps to give them an otherworldly quality, or perhaps suggests that fate is unavoidable. Their four-beat line is also fitting for spells and incantations:

• **When** | shall **we** | three **meet** | a**gain**, (1.1.1)

Shakespeare also uses rhyme for the ends of scenes, where a 'rhyming couplet' can have the effect of rounding things off, as it does in 1.7.

Find the other scenes which end with a rhyming couplet and discuss what the effect might be in each case.

Verse and prose

It is never totally clear why Shakespeare chooses to write some scenes, or passages, in verse, and others in prose. Although there are many examples where the more serious scenes, involving great passions, are in verse while those about ordinary people and comedy are in prose, there are also significant examples throughout Shakespeare's plays where this is not the case.

In 1.5, Macbeth's letter, read out by his wife, is in prose (1–13), but her responses to it are in verse; the porter speaks in prose, but Macduff seems to be replying in verse (2.3.1–44); the Murderers speak in verse (3.3), but the doctor and gentlewoman in prose (5.1); Lady Macduff switches from verse to prose in the same scene (4.2); Lady Macbeth usually speaks in verse, but her sleepwalking scene is in prose (5.1).

Discuss the uses of prose in *Macbeth*, a play which is very largely in verse.
Is there any rule which can be drawn up about when prose is used?

The plot of *Macbeth*

Act 1

1.1: The Witches plan when they will meet Macbeth.

1.2: A soldier reports to King Duncan that the rebel Macdonwald and his
Norwegian allies have been defeated after acts of great valour by the
Scottish generals, Banquo and Macbeth. Duncan sentences the Thane of
Cawdor to death and declares that Macbeth will be given the title.

1.3: Returning from the battle, Macbeth and Banquo are accosted by the
Witches who address Macbeth as Thane of Glamis, Thane of Cawdor and
'king hereafter', and inform Banquo that his descendants will be kings but
he himself will not. As the Witches vanish, Rosse arrives to tell Macbeth that
he has been made Thane of Cawdor and, while Banquo warns that Witches
sometimes try to lure us to evil, Macbeth sees this news as indicating that
the second prophecy – that he will be king – might also come true, a thought
which disturbs him greatly. He resolves to leave matters to chance.

1.4: Duncan thanks Macbeth for his part in defeating the rebels, but
confounds Macbeth's plans to be king by announcing that his son Malcolm
is to be his heir. Macbeth begins to plot how he can overcome this obstacle
to his ambitions.

1.5: Lady Macbeth reads a letter from her husband in which he tells her
about the Witches' prophecies. She fears that he is too good-natured to kill
Duncan and decides to use all her powers to persuade him. Receiving
news that Duncan plans to spend that night in the Macbeths' castle, she
calls upon evil spirits to harden herself for the impending murder. When
Macbeth arrives, he seems reluctant to say much and Lady Macbeth
advises him to look innocent but leave the rest to her.

1.6: Duncan and Banquo arrive at the castle and are admiring its
attractiveness when Lady Macbeth comes to welcome them with words of
obedience and loyalty.

1.7: Leaving the banquet, Macbeth expresses his doubts about murdering
Duncan and fights with his conscience: he fears the judgement of the
afterlife and knows that a host should protect his guest, especially a king

who has been as virtuous and just as Duncan. He has no incentive for killing him except his own ambition, and, when Lady Macbeth comes to fetch him back into the banquet, he declares that they will not proceed with their murderous plans. Calling him a coward, taunting him with not being a real man, and showing how she would never go back upon an oath, Lady Macbeth persuades her husband and explains how the blame for the murder can be laid upon Duncan's guards.

Act 2

2.1: Duncan has retired for the night and Macbeth tests Banquo to see how loyal he might be in the future. Left alone, Macbeth has a vision of a bloodstained dagger and, hearing a bell, goes to kill Duncan.

2.2: Lady Macbeth has drugged the guards and says she might have killed Duncan herself had he not resembled her father as he slept. Macbeth enters and reports that he has done the deed, but is disturbed by having heard a voice telling him that he will now sleep no more. She is appalled to see that he has brought the bloody daggers with him and, as he is too frightened to take them back to Duncan's chamber, she does it. There is a knocking on the castle door and they leave the scene to wash the blood away, Macbeth wishing that the continued knocking could wake the King.

2.3: The castle porter pretends that he is the porter of hell-gate and imagines some of the people who might come his way. After finally opening the door to Macduff and Lenox, he talks about the effects of drink, at which point Macbeth enters to greet them and Macduff goes to wake the King. As Lenox reports the strange sights and noises experienced during the night, Macduff screams out the horrifying news of the King's murder and others arrive, including Banquo, Lady Macbeth and the King's two sons, Malcolm and Donalbain. The evidence points to the guards, but Macduff is not the only person to be suspicious that Macbeth has killed them and Lady Macbeth's faint usefully draws people's attention away from her husband. Malcolm and Donalbain, suspecting treachery, decide privately to escape abroad.

2.4: An old man and Rosse discuss the strange, unnatural events that have followed Duncan's murder and Macduff joins them to express his cynicism at the allegations that the guards had been in the pay of Malcolm and Donalbain. While Macduff resolves to return to his home castle in Fife, Rosse goes to see Macbeth crowned in Scone.

Act 3

3.1: Banquo privately expresses his suspicions about Macbeth but recalls that their prophecies declared that he would be the ancestor of many kings. Macbeth and Lady Macbeth – now King and Queen – welcome him, and Macbeth checks that Banquo intends to go out riding and take his son Fleance with him. Macbeth announces that Duncan's sons are spreading slanderous rumours about him and then privately expresses his fears about Banquo and his torment at the fact that he has committed a grave sin only to benefit Banquo and his heirs. He then persuades two Murderers to kill Banquo and Fleance, explaining that Banquo had always been their enemy, and presenting him as a threat to himself.

3.2: When Lady Macbeth asks her husband why he is keeping himself to himself, he explains that there are dangers remaining and he is tormented by the thought of Banquo and the prophecy, but that he has matters in hand. Refusing to confide in her, he tells her that evil deeds need to be reinforced by further crimes.

3.3: A third Murderer joins the other two, but the assassination is botched: they kill Banquo, but Fleance escapes.

3.4: That night Macbeth entertains the lords at a banquet. One of the Murderers comes to report what has happened and Macbeth is appalled to hear that Fleance got away. Turning to take his seat, he sees Banquo's bloody ghost and, despite all Lady Macbeth's efforts to calm him, he suspiciously betrays all his terror, and the banquet ends in disarray. Totally unnerved by the vision, Macbeth decides to visit the Witches the next day and know the worst that may befall: from now on he will act swiftly and violently.

3.5: The Witch goddess, Hecate, is angry with the Witches for failing to involve her in their dealings with Macbeth, but arranges to see them the following morning before their next meeting with Macbeth, whose overconfidence she promises to punish.

3.6: Lenox ironically describes Macbeth's tyrannous actions to another lord, who reports that Macduff has fled to England where Malcolm is being sheltered by the King, Edward the Confessor. Macduff, who had earlier refused to see Macbeth, is seeking English support to overthrow him.

Act 4

4.1: Macbeth visits the Witches once more and demands that they answer his questions, no matter what the consequences might be. The Witches' spirit masters conjure up three apparitions: the first, a head wearing armour, tells him to beware Macduff; the second, a bloody child, tells him that he need fear no man 'of woman born'; the third, a child wearing a crown and carrying a tree, informs him that he will never be defeated until Birnam wood comes against him. Taking comfort from these prophecies, he asks whether Banquo's descendants will ever be kings in Scotland and is reluctantly answered by a vision representing the eight Stewart kings including James, all presided over by Banquo. As the Witches and the apparitions disappear, Lenox arrives to bring news that Macduff has fled to England, and Macbeth resolves instantly to attack his castle and kill all its inhabitants.

4.2: Rosse rushes to Fife to warn Lady Macduff, who is angry at her husband's action in leaving her and his family vulnerable. As Rosse leaves and she discusses with her son what a traitor is, a terrified messenger arrives and tells her to flee immediately. But it is too late, and she and her children are brutally murdered.

4.3: Macduff has arrived in England and attempts to persuade Malcolm to return to Scotland and help overthrow Macbeth. Malcolm is suspicious – Macbeth has tried to entrap him before – and tests Macduff by pretending that, were he to become king, Scotland would have an even more wicked tyrant on the throne than Macbeth. Initially Macduff argues that this does not matter, but, as Malcolm's stories of his sins increase in seriousness, Macduff begins to despair. This is the confirmation that Malcolm has been looking for and he reveals that he has been inventing these stories against himself to test Macduff's loyalty; he has an army to support him and is ready to invade. They are discussing the English King's ability to cure the sick, when Rosse arrives and, after reporting rumours that the Scots are beginning to rise against Macbeth, he breaks the news to Macduff of his family's cruel slaughter. Malcolm tries to comfort Macduff, who feels to blame for their deaths, and they prepare to invade.

Act 5

5.1: A doctor and a gentlewoman watch Lady Macbeth sleepwalking, now a common occurrence. She seems to think she is washing the blood from her hands and her words give evidence that her mind has been disturbed by guilt and the horror of the murders that have taken place.

5.2: Lenox and other Scottish lords are seen marching to join Malcolm and the English army near Birnam wood and they discuss reports that Macbeth has taken refuge in Dunsinane, troubled by his conscience and followed out of fear, not loyalty.

5.3: In Dunsinane castle, Macbeth refuses to hear any more reports, confident that he cannot be harmed. He dismisses a report that there are ten thousand English approaching, but broods at the thought that, in old age, he can expect only hatred. The doctor reports that Lady Macbeth is diseased in her mind and Macbeth prepares to fight, armed with the Witches' predictions.

5.4: Arriving at Birnam wood, Malcolm orders every man to cut down a bough, in order to disguise the size of their army, and hears that many of Macbeth's former followers have deserted.

5.5: Macbeth waits for the attack, confident that Dunsinane can withstand a siege, but his armourer Seyton brings news that Lady Macbeth has died and this prompts Macbeth to thoughts about the shortness and pointlessness of life. His earlier confidence in the Witches' prophecies receives a blow when news comes that Birnam wood appears to be moving, but he resolves at least to die fighting.

5.6: As the English army approaches, Malcolm gives the responsibility of leading the attack to Siward, Earl of Northumberland, and to Siward's son.

5.7: The battle begins and Macbeth, feeling now like a bear being baited, kills Young Siward. Macduff, however, is tracking him down. The castle surrenders and Old Siward invites Malcolm to enter.

5.8: Macbeth is finally confronted by Macduff, the one opponent he would rather have avoided. His confident boast about his invulnerability to any man born of woman is dashed when Macduff reveals his Caesarean birth. But Macbeth refuses to suffer the humiliation that would follow surrender and fights on.

5.9: Malcolm and his English allies are victorious, Siward's brave son the only notable casualty. Macduff enters with Macbeth's head on a pole and Malcolm ends the play by making his loyal thanes into Scotland's first earls and inviting them to attend his coronation at Scone.

Study skills: titles and quotations

Referring to titles

When you are writing an essay, you will often need to refer to the title of the play. There are two main ways of doing this:

- If you are handwriting your essay, the title of the play should be underlined:
  <u>Macbeth</u>.
- If you are word-processing your essay, the play title should be in italics:
  Macbeth.

The same rules apply to titles of all plays and other long works including novels and non-fiction, such as: *Animal Farm* and *The Diary of Anne Frank*. The titles of poems or short stories are placed inside single inverted commas; for example: 'Timothy Winters' and 'A Sound of Thunder'.

Note that the first word in a title and all the main words will have capital (or 'upper case') letters, while the less important words (such as conjunctions, prepositions and articles) will usually begin with lower case letters; for example: *The Taming of the Shrew or Antony and Cleopatra.*

Using quotations

Quotations show that you know the play in detail and are able to produce evidence from the script to back up your ideas and opinions. It is usually a good idea to keep quotations as short as you can (and this especially applies to exams, where it is a waste of time copying chunks out of the script).

Using long quotations

There are a number of things you should do if you want to use a quotation of more than a few words:

Background to Shakespeare

1. Make your point. ——— **The witches dramatically establish the world of the play:**

2. A colon introduces the quotation.

3. Leave a line ———————

4. Indent the quotation. ——— **Fair is foul, and foul is fair:**

5. No quotation marks.

6. Keep the same line-divisions as the script. ——— **Hover through the fog . . .**

7. Three dots show that the quotation is incomplete.

8. Continue with a follow-up point, perhaps commenting on the quotation itself. ——— **Their incantation prepares us for . . .**

Using brief quotations

Brief quotations are usually easier to use, take less time to write out and are much more effective in showing how familiar you are with the play. Embed them in the sentence like this:

- Lady Macbeth's fear that her husband's nature is 'too full o' the milk of human kindness' suggests that she . . .

If you are asked to state where the quotation comes from, use this simple form of reference:

- Malcolm's description of Macbeth as 'this dead butcher' (5.9.35) emphasises not only . . .

In some editions this is written partly in Roman numerals – upper case for the Act and lower case for the scene; for example: (V.ix.35), or (V.9.35).

William Shakespeare and *Macbeth*

We do not know exactly when *Macbeth* was written, but it is possible to make a reasonable assumption that it was some time in 1606. It must have been written after the execution of the equivocator Father Garnet in May 1606 (because of the Porter's references to the event) and must have been performed by 1607, because other plays from that year refer to the scene in which Banquo's ghost appears. In fact, the first performance might have been before King James himself at Hampton Court on 7 August 1606.

Shakespeare's life and career

No one is absolutely sure when he wrote each play.

1564   Born in Stratford-upon-Avon, first son of John and Mary Shakespeare.
1582   Marries Anne Hathaway from the nearby village of Shottery. She is eight years older and expecting their first child.
1583   Daughter Susanna born.
1585   Twin son and daughter, Hamnet and Judith, born.

Some time before 1592 Shakespeare arrives in London, becomes an actor and writes poems and plays. Several plays are performed, probably including the three parts of *Henry VI*. Another writer, Robert Greene, writes about 'Shake-scene', the 'upstart crow' who has clearly become a popular playwright.

By March 1595 he is a shareholder with the Lord Chamberlain's Men (see page 194) and has probably written *Richard III*, *Comedy of Errors*, *Titus Andronicus*, *Taming of the Shrew*, *Two Gentlemen of Verona*, *Love's Labour's Lost*, *Romeo and Juliet*, *Richard II* and *A Midsummer Night's Dream* (as well as contributing to plays by other writers and writing the poems 'Venus and Adonis' and 'The Rape of Lucrece').

1596   Hamnet dies, aged 11.
1597   Buys New Place, one of the finest houses in Stratford.
1599   Globe theatre opens on Bankside.

By 1599: *King John*, *Merchant of Venice*, the two parts of *Henry IV*, *Merry Wives of Windsor*, *Much Ado About Nothing*, *Julius Caesar* and *Henry V* (as well as the Sonnets).

1603   King James I grants the Lord Chamberlain's Men a Royal Patent and they become the King's Men (page 199).

By 1608: *As You Like It*, *Hamlet*, *Twelfth Night*, *Troilus and Cressida*, *All's Well That Ends Well*, *Measure for Measure*, *Othello*, *Macbeth*, *King Lear*, *Antony and Cleopatra*, *Pericles*, *Coriolanus* and *Timon of Athens*.

1608   The King's Men begin performing plays in the indoor Blackfriars theatre (page 193).

By 1613: *Cymbeline*, *The Winter's Tale*, *The Tempest*, *Henry VIII*, *Two Noble Kinsmen* (the last two probably with John Fletcher).

1613   Globe theatre destrayed by fire.
1614   The rebuilt Globe theatre opens.
1616   Dies, 23 April, and is buried in Holy Trinity Church, Stratford.
1623   Publication of the First Folio (page 195).

Shakespeare's times

1558   Elizabeth I becomes queen.
1565   The sailor John Hawkins introduces sweet potatoes and tobacco into England.
1567   Mary Queen of Scots is forced to abdicate in favour of her year-old son, James VI.
1567   The first-known playhouse in London, the Red Lion, is built.
1568   Mary escapes to England and is imprisoned by Elizabeth.
1572   Francis Drake attacks Spanish ports in the Americas.
1576   James Burbage opens the Theatre in London.
1580   Francis Drake returns from the first English circumnavigation of the world.
1582   Pope Gregory reforms the Christian calendar.
1587   Mary Queen of Scots executed for a treasonous plot against Elizabeth; Drake destroys two dozen Spanish ships at Cadiz and war breaks out with Spain.
1588   Philip II of Spain's Armada is defeated by the English fleet.
1593   Plague kills 11,000 Londoners.
1593   Playwright Christopher Marlowe killed in a pub brawl.
1595   The Earl of Tyrone leads a new rebellion in Ireland.
1596   Tomatoes introduced into England; John Harington invents the water-closet (the ancestor of the modern lavatory).
1599   The Earl of Essex concludes a truce with Tyrone, returns home and is arrested.
1601   Essex is tried and executed for treasonous plots against Elizabeth.
1603   Elizabeth I dies and is succeeded by James VI of Scotland as James I of England.
1603   Sir Walter Raleigh is jailed for plotting against James.
1604   James is proclaimed 'King of Great Britain, France and Ireland'; new Church rules cause 300 Puritan clergy to resign.
1605   Gunpowder Plot uncovered.
1607   First permanent English settlement in America at Jamestown, Virginia.

1610 Galileo looks at the stars through a telescope; tea is introduced into Europe.
1611 The Authorised Version of the Bible published.
1618 Raleigh executed; physician William Harvey announces discovery of blood circulation.
1620 Pilgrim Fathers sail from Plymouth to colonise America.
1625 James I dies and is succeeded by Charles I.

Index of activities